The **Homefulness Handbook**

How to Build a Homeless & Landless People's Solution to Homelessness

Visioned, lived & written by
POOR Magazine Family

Book design, and typesetting: A.S. Ikeda
Cover art: Tiburcio Garcia
Cover design: A.S. Ikeda

Thank you to the POOR Magazine admin team for editing support, and to Mama Earth, Homefulness, POOR Magazine and Deecolonzie Academy Liberated Villages and all of our ancestors

You can get our books and online curriculum at
www.poormagazine.org
www.poorpress.net

A Note from the POOR Press Linguistic Liberation Team

As you read this beautiful POOR Press book, please understand that as colonized and oppressed peoples in poverty, we do not speak the colonizer's languages with academic precision. We resist linguistic domination by writing and speaking and creating. There will be typos and different uses of language. These are our voives, our art, and our resistance narratives. Read them with love and spirit in your hearts. Decolonize your mind one page at a time.

The photos in this book are of varying quality and size, and we chose to include them as they are. We believe this honors poverty skolas and the realities of poverty journalism. It was more important to preserve the photos as documentation rather than leave them out, and we believe the book is better because these images are included.

We must thank Creator for another day of Life—
Ancestors of this Ohlone/Lisjan Land for allowing
us to be here and watching over us every day and
still being here 528 years later. Thank my sisSTAR
Laure McElroy, my mama Dee and all the ancestors
of poverty, homelessness, poLice terror, coloniza-
tion and the violence of sweeps and to all of us at
Homefulness and POOR Magazine who never stop
fighting, always keep writing into being the UnSelling
of Mama Earth until we can Homefulness the World...

Acknowledgments

Tiny Gray-Garcia

Acknowledge first and foremost sisSTAR Corrina Gould and Fuifuilupe Niumeitolu and their ancestors for giving us permission and spiritual guidance to be here and helping us along the way prayerfully, spiritually and lovingly. To my Mama Dee for without whom there would be no me, her vision, her art and deep poverty scholarship and for surviving her life of extreme poverty, abuse, torture, struggle and isolation and teaching me to know so clearly what must be done to heal all of us caught in the krapitalist violence of this stolen land.

To all the survivors, victims and ancestors of landlessness, homelessness, racism, redlining, gentriFUKation, colonial theft, extraction, evictions and poLice terror of Mama Earth who never stop giving up, fighting or resisting, and finally to all the victims of sweeps and cleaning up and poLice terror who have died because being houseless and landless is a crime on this stolen land.

To all the mentees, POOR Magazine solidarity family who learned and listened carefully to us poverty skolaz and radically redistributed their stolen and hoarded resources so we houseless, indigenous, landless poverty skolaz could even MamaFest this powerFULL vision.

And to Mama Earth for without whom there would be no we...

Contents

3. Poverty Skolaz' Stories & Poems

4. Bloodstained into Lovestained Bucks

5. Tools for Mama Earth Liberation

Introduction

Tiny Gray-Garcia

From LandBack to Black Land—from the Lie of Discovery to the Settler Colonial Lie of Private Property—From the Black Panthers to MOVE Africa, Zapatistas to Sogorea Te' Land Trust to Homefulness Land Trust in WHAT??

How do poor, houseless indigenous, evicted, disabled, false-border-terrorized peoples from all four corners of Mama Earth, now residing on stolen and occupied Turtle Island, who have been displaced, evicted, incarcerated, swept, criminalized and traumatized actually "buy" land and build permanent homes, food justice, art and healing comeUnity for themselves and the world?

The question almost seems unanswerable. This vision seems almost unrealizable in a krapitalist system, whose entire criminal injustice system is set up to protect the settler lie of private property. But this lie must be unpacked. These myths and messages of hoarding, accumulating, buying, selling, evicting, incarcerating, sweeping and stealing must be unTold and unLearned. Mama Earth is not now and has never been for sale, and our indigenous ancestors have always taught us that. We must learn, write and live it back.

Through layers of what we call Poverty Scholarship in Practice—i.e., with permission and guidance from First Nations peoples, talk-story, poetry, theatre, education, All Nations prayer and ceremony with ancestors and Mama Earth, Poor peoples of all colors and nations working together with humility, love, realness and self-determined vision, extremely hard work and commitment to each other, while simultaneously teaching/working with conscious wealth-hoarders, akkkademikly privileged and papered and stolen land inheritors—it can be done.

This book is the journey and the how-to of the powerFULL poverty skolaz and ancestors of POOR Magazine spiritually and legally unselling Mama Earth and building the vision that is Homefulness. This books takes you through the unfolding in real time, with all the hard parts, gray areas, and UnClarity that MamaFestation (as I call it) means in a stolen land of lies and in this moment when Mama Earth, Mama Ocean, Father Sky and all of our four-legged and winged relatives are under attack, so angry, so CorpRaped and so hurt.

And the deadly, violent and evil "solution" of the War on the Poor, perpetrated by politricks and wealth-hoarders rages on, leading to the death of unhoused and poor people all across Mama Earth.

This book is dedicated to Shannon Marie Bigley, Desiree Quintero and Papa Bear and all the unknown Soldiers who have died from the violence called sweeps and the lie called Private Property....and is a how-to HumblePrayer, a gift and a love message to Mama Earth and all of us. Please read, pray and learn with an open heart and a humble mind. Ometeotl, Ase, Semign Cacona Guari, Ahoo.

P.S. We will come to your town, encampment, street corner, church or school and teach on this book thru Zoom or in person. Please contact poormag@gmail.com for more information.

Chapter 1
Roots

The HER-Story of Homefulness

Tiny Gray-Garcia

There is a house in East Huchuin
They Call it Homefulness
And its been the dream of many a poor girl
And God I know im one

My mama was disabled
Tortured as a child
My father was a rich wite man
Who left us all to die

Now the only thing a poor mama needs
Are hands to hold her dreams
But mama and me were all alone
So instead we lived on the street

mama and me were broken
Barely made it out alive
but no matter what
She refused to believe in the
settler colonial lies

Sometimes the pain is too hard
Mama said I can't go on
But walk this change
On this Ohlone land
And Build us all a home

Well there is a house in East Huchuin
They call it Homefulness
And its been the hope of many a poor girl & boy
And GOD I know we are them

Well there is a house in East Huchuin
They call HOMEFULNESS

And its been the dream of many a poor boy & girl
And god I know we are them...

The door to our nylon tent was flapping violently. We had found a secluded place in Golden Gate park after having our last hooptie (old broke-down car) towed. We stayed in a motel for two luxurious days, then ended up back on the street in Downtown Oakland, and then one morning we were "swept" from that location.

Now we were here. We thought we were "safe" at least for a few days, but then we noticed the park ranger was surveilling us. We tried to keep silent but the wind was betraying us.

Five more sweeps and tent seizures, one more hotel stay and a temporary storefront squat later, we got another hooptie. This was a station wagon and once again, we had no money, skills or ability to get it "smogged" so it remained unregistered. Two months later it was towed and we were back in the tent.

This impossible cycle of temporary, sort of housing, poverty crimes of being unhoused, belonging theft, and outside living began when I was 11. Mamá lost her job and became disabled and this went on for years, into my adulthood. It was necessary I drop out of school and enroll full-time in the Skool of hard knocks aka survival.

My mama, a disabled mixed race single parent poverty skola who had survived torture at the hands of foster parents and orphanages as a "ward of the court" and life on the streets of North Philadelphia and a marriage to my abusive, entitled, colonizer dad, could not really change our situation. Neither could 11, 12, 13, 14, 15, 16, 17, or 18 year old me. No matter how hard we worked at it. We had a street-based, unlicensed micro-business selling art, which we worked really hard at but never seemed to get "ahead" or on top or any of the other krapitalist lies of success that get thrown at poor people. No matter how hard we try.

Homefulness Hooptie Parking

While we had that last station wagon hooptie, we parked wherever people wouldn't call the poLice. Where at least it was hard to be seen or more importantly noticed. One day we ended up on MacArthur

Houseless

By Tiburcio Garcia, 12, Youth Skola with
Deecolonize Academy at POOR Magazine

On the sidewalk the pounding of feet passing by. We holding up cardboard signs and all we usually get a wary eye. Always moving. People think we looting. We are treated like criminals for sleeping on the street even though America is the one who made sure we had nothing to eat. This country left us jobless, friendless, loveless, and most of all houseless.

Blvd., in deep East Oakland (what we later named BlackArthur, in what we later learned was occupied Deep East Huchuin). We were in front of the post office, a weirdly quiet stretch of road, in the middle of the hood.

It was in that car, on that stretch of BlackArthur that me and mama conceived of the notion of Homefulness. It wasn't new or different. We weren't the only poor people who knew that the violence of isolation kills, that the lie of rent kills, that sweeps kill, and inter-dependence gives life and support and love. WE talked for hours about our impossible struggle and about a dream that included equity, stability, roofs, and healing. And of course, it all seemed like an impossible dream. No one was listening to the solutions of a poor disabled, houseless mama and daughter living on the street.

We parked here for months, unseen, until one day we made the mistake of driving to Berkeley to "celebrate my birthday." We never made it back.

We were stopped, told to get out of the unregistered car, thrown against the wall, and arrested for the act of accruing too many citations for the act of being houseless. The car—which was my mama's only place to sleep—and all of our remaining belongings were towed. I was in county jail for 3 months and came out only because of a revolutionary lawyer who uses his law degree and class privilege in the revolutionary service of poor and houseless people.

No Matter How Many Times you incarcerate me—it doesn't give me a home…

Incarcerating me for the 'crime' of being houseless didn't make me "homeful" it just increased our hopelessness. Why I always say no matter how many times you incarcerate, study, or sweep me, it doesn't give me a home….

When I got out of jail, me and mama were done. My poor mama was always depressed because of her severe PTSD, but this was different. We were done in a way that was almost unspeakable. The ways that so many of us become when, as mama used to say, we could not survive one more little murder of the soul.

I tried to take my life. It was not successful. It would not be the last time. The depression, the loss and the inability to change your situation kills your very soul. I know y'all poverty skolaz reading this feel me. Others, take our collective word for it. It is why so many of us begin self-medicating, losing our minds and our intractable situations in whatever way we can. Just so we don't have to remember, re-live, and continue to feel the hurt we cannot change.

The Three interventions (Miracles)

Eventually, my fierce, never giving up Mama (and me, always at her side as her support person, good daughter) began to audit classes in all the consciousness that had been successfully colonized away from her. Black Studies, Raza Studies, Women's Studies, Indigenous Studies. Together we began to learn that we weren't alone, that poor families in struggle all across Mama Earth shared a lot of our same experiences. Eviction, poverty, homelessness, and disability were not our fault. We began to stop internalizing the krapitalist narrative about how bad our choices had been and we began writing a resistance narrative. This was the beginning of our political consciousness.

Next, I encountered an Indigenous landlord who didn't evict us when we didn't have all the rent money and instead saw me as "a good daughter." And lastly, that revolutionary lawyer I mentioned transformed my several thousand hours of community service into a writing assignment. For the first time in my life I even considered myself a "writer" (the deeper details of these moments were included in the book I wrote in honor of my mama and all the generations of poor broken women I come from, called *Criminal of Poverty: Growing Up Homeless in America*).

Over time with our newer, clearer consciousness and a tiny sliver of hope, we launched POOR Magazine street-writing workshops while still struggling with homelessness and criminalization ourselves.

We held revolutionary poor people-led writing workshops in shelters, bus stops, street corners, and welfare offices. A year later, after so much innovative hustle and flow, work and support from well-known installation artists like Evri Kwong who believed in our vision, we actually published a hard copy of a dream. A glossy, art-filled magazine written, edited, and published by poor and houseless folks focused on our own solutions to our problems. The first solution was our answer to homelessness we called *Homefulness*.

There were so many more stories of our survival and the launching of the organization of the same name that can be read and followed in the *Criminal of Poverty* book and the *Poverty Scholarship* textbook. But for now I will say that one of the most important "lessons" we learned in this time was the violence of rich people defined as "charity" and all of the lies inherent in what I later dubbed the Charity Industrial Complex.

Whenever me and my mama got a charity crumb we did what all poor people always do, share it immediately with our fellow poor folks, however and wherever we could.

I had taught myself to write grants and we were able to get the first and only grant in the nation teaching poor families journalism. But we wouldn't "report" aka criminalize fellow poor people when they were late or absent to our classes, because we knew that poverty skolaz are always late and absent because we have so much PTSD and responsibilities just in the job of survival while poor.

Again so many urgent lessons of Poverty Scholarship that people who might have trouble with these concepts can learn in the Poverty Scholarship textbook and/or by attending one of our PeopleSkool seminars.

The abbreviated version of this particular horror story is that one year later the City and County pulled every single cent from us and all the private "Charities" who had also "supported" our innovative model of poor people teaching/learning life-changing, followed suit.

They put us through hell and once again it broke my mama's spirit and the Indigenous poor people-led movement of POOR Magazine, intrinsically entwined with all of us poor people leaders, ended up broke and houseless again.

Mama ended up getting sick with what took her to the other side of the spirit journey. I got pregnant and was eventually caught in multiple struggles of ghetto drama of Domestic Violence and trauma and homelessness.

But we held on to POOR Magazine by any means necessary. For Poor folks, all we know is to hold on tight. We kept trying things, like HUD grants to "fund" Homefulness. And there were more krapitalist business plans led by rich people who were doing "charity" by "helping" us poor people. But never having missed a meal themselves and never listening or learning Poverty Scholarship, they instead set up hurting systems of "help" that were set-ups from the get-ups. With every turn we were rejected, turned down, disrespected, or mis-guided, questioned for our legitimacy and disbelieved.

The Herstory of Mamahouse

MamaHouse was the baby-dream of Homefulness. Mamahouse, the revolutionary concept and project launched by my Mama Dee and me so many years ago as a collective for mothers and children in poverty. It was a place to live and resist the deep isolation that kills the spirits of so many people in a capitalist society, combat the discrimination that impacts poor single parents of color, and provide peer support and scholarship for the struggle of raising a child in this society that never supports poor parents and has effectively separated our elders and ancestors from our young folks. Mamahouse, a collective living space for houseless single parents and children that we rented with all kinds of code-switching and lies to scamlords, me "leveraging" aka using my skin privilege for racist, classist code-switch success, to support each other as poor mamaz in trauma with all of the support this society never gives you.

Mamahouse has always worked, even as capitalism hasn't. In its first incarnation, Mamahouse existed within a tiny one-bedroom apartment in the Tenderloin District, launched by a revolutionary slice of philan-thro-pimped dollars, meant solely for a series of writing workshops with youth, adults, and elders in poverty and the publication of Volume 1 of POOR Magazine, which was called HOMEFULNESS. The work-shops and publication were done with great success, at which point my revolutionary, community-driven, always tortured by capitalism, Indigenous Taino, single mama of color in poverty, Dee, announced in an act of change-By-Any-Means-Necessary!, "Let's realize the dream of Homefulness beyond the pages, otherwise we may never see it happen."

My beautiful and sad mama, stripped, separated, and devoid of her Indigenous family, culture, language and community, never took anything for granted. She always knew, like all us po' folks know, that if you ever have any access or money that there is absolutely no guarantee that it will continue to be there or continue to flow, no matter how hard you pull up your bootstraps or dream the only-in-sleep-Amer-ikkklan Dream.

And as soon as we had a few resources to realize any dreams of counter-capitalism-separate-ness, we did.

It was never easy, we were never supported in our efforts, but we knew if we were to infiltrate the destruction of capitalist separatism in real time, in our own lives, as a poor single mama of color and daughter, with no extended family or community, it was necessary that we act fast and act revolutionarily.

I work so hard in my mind and heart everyday to not take my son through the sorrow of loneliness, desperation, and poverty that me and my mama felt for so many years. Isolation kills. Capitalism promotes isolation and the cult of independence and separation. Our barometer for sanity is based on how "happy" we can be while being alone, separate from others and at peace with our solitude.

The Tenderloin Mamahouse, circa 1998, successfully housed two landless Indigenous families, ran beautiful community dinners and art events, and silly moments of love and Indigenous justice in real time.

We had to end it one year later, due to no more funding. Sadly, capital campaigns (property acquisitions) are usually only launched

and realized by already-wealthy organizations and individuals who have access to long ago stolen-from Indigenous peoples' U.S. resources.

In 2005, after a series of very serious organizational and personal losses at POOR Magazine, (organizational and personal lives are naturally enmeshed as a natural part of revolutionary poor people-led/Indigenous people-led organizations like ours), I founded the next series of Mamahouses. This one in a substandard house in the Mission District, shared with many non-paying tenants with tails and feathers and wings and antennas. These un-seen tenants facilitated the only truly affordable market rate housing in the brutally gentrified Mission District of San Francisco.

In 2007, the slumlord from hell of this Mamahouse actually set fire to her own property to rid her building of "problem tenants" like us mamas and children. In other words, tenants that tried to get her to fix the plumbing and rid the house of the serious rat, roach, and pigeon infestation. It proved one of my other theories—that poor folks who want/need to stay have to take substandard dangerous conditions like mold, insect infestation, and asbestos, even if it kills us, just to remain housed.

Which brought us to Mamahouse #3—the Gentrification Palace—an unbelievably beautiful place with shining floors and spacious rooms and a backyard out of the pages of a glossy magazine, only affordable to us poor mamaz because one of the mamaz had a housing subsidy.

"Mama, can we stay here forever?" my son would ask while we lived within its serene structure with multiple other mamaz in and out of crisis, several children, a houseless family member or two, birds, cats, and even a little dog sharing stories, dreams, ideas, and equity, crafting complex future plans for Homefulness's truly shared equity and food localization, and a micro-business economic self-sustainability model.

And then one day it was over. The slice of paper hung flimsily from the grand blue oak door. "60-Day Notice." Its words slashing across the page, dripped with ancient blood of conquistadors, missionaries, real estate speculators, mortgage brokers, developers, and benevolent landlords. My relationship with its beauty, it's never-really-mine-stability, its community with other mamaz and families, life-breathing support and love was gone.

On our last day at Mamahouse, all of us Indigenous mamaz, brothers, sons, daughters, uncles, aunties, grandmothers, and grandfathers huddled together with our abuelita pictures, icons, and spirits from our mama altars, our clothing, stuffies, beds, desks, chairs, wastebaskets, feathers, icons, beads, shoes, and toys strewn across the sidewalk, scattered from the wind-less hurricane of deadly gentrification and displacement while default gentrifiers raced by to get $4.00 fair-trade, organic, coffee and raw, vegan donuts at the plethora of blonde wood filled cafes and $100 artist/designer dresses at the new, "underground" clothing stores beginning to fill up all the store-fronts in our inner-Mission neighborhood.

My eyes cry tears of untold evictions and displacement of communities—of children and elders—faces that are left in faded murals to be covered in sheets of cold white paint or brushed over by the whimsical brush strokes of hipster/artists that have no respect for the neighborhoods they gentrify.

As the rays of warm Mission sun began to slip away through our beloved, no longer ours, front yard tree, all us mamas and children were still pulling thing after tragic thing out of unseen crevasses in the house.

All of sudden, my son, perched on a box full of his complete collection of Legos, looked up at me, tilting his head to the side and holding back tears, "Mama, it's ok, I just figured it out. We are going to move to Homefulness after this and then we will all be ok."

Remembering, always recollecting the words of the Po' Poet Laureate of POOR Magazine, A. Faye Hicks, "When us po folk are evicted we don't always leave the neighborhood, we just move into the sidewalk hotels, the card-board hotels, the street."

A group of poverty skolaz—adults and children—stands in front of Mamahouse, a few of them with their fists in the air. Tiny holds a sign that says "No more evictions."

Happy Houseless Mamaz Day

When People Say
Happy Mamas day
it jus never felt ok

When so many mamas & babies sit behind false borders and
  steel bars,
sleeping in tents and cars,
Dreaming of their lost babies shot by PoLice fire
No equity, No Money,
Not time to love or spit bars
Hold their babies in their arms
Dream Dreams or Gaze at stars
Our Communities and support and life lost to gentriFUKED
  streets
Our ideas and dreams so often Silenced so we can barely
  speak
Happy Mamas Day...
How can it really be –
anything more than Amerikkklan Hypocrisy
How bout Equity, Healing-Care Not HellthCare
How bout Housing, De-carceration and the end of PoLice
  Terror of our Suns and Daughters and the War on the
  POOR
Happy Mamaz Day
How can it be
Until all of our Mamas & Mama Earth Can b free
Otherwise isn't Happy Mamas Day just more krapitalist
  HypKRAZY?

The document said "30 day notice to pay a $700 rent increase or quit."

The white paper with the oversized violent black font fluttered in the morning breeze. We three houseless, disabled mamas sat huddled at a long wooden table in the huge kitchen at MamaHouse #3 in San Francisco's dangerously gentrifying Mission District—where the word gentriFUKation originated from my mouth, born out of my anger and sorrow for the violent plight of so many poor folks dealing with displacement. The bright morning sun streaming through beautiful long windows warmed our terrorized faces.

"I knew it, this place was too nice for us, it was just a matter of time," Laure McElroy, my longtime sister, mama warrior, fellow Po'

poet and founding member of POOR Magazine 's welfareQUEEN's project with me and other poor mamas, crumpled up the notice and then un-crumpled it. The pace of her voice sped up like it always did when she got triggered by fear of homelessness.

"$700?"

Sandra Sandoval, long-time Mission district resident, organizer, and the 3rd fierce mama who struggled with homelessness with her infant son before she moved into MamaHouse with me and Laure, shook her head at the notice.

In September of 2010, all of us mamas were scattered to the wind by that eviction from MamaHouse and sitting outside our beautiful ex-home on Florida Street. We were houseless with all of our children and our belongings in hefty bags on the sidewalk.

"I miss MamaHouse so much," Laure whispered to me a year after the eviction when she was struggling to get some stable housing. She passed away in August 2018, a victim of the compound trauma of houselessness, poverty, isolation, and depression.

She never recovered from that eviction. Most of us don't.

"Where is my Mother's Day card?" Mama asked me one Mother's Day when we were struggling with yet another eviction notice in yet another apartment. This time, the fear was worse, I was pregnant with my soon to be born son.

"Mother's Day is a CONsumer lie," I replied angrily. "How can we celebrate when things are so bad for us, for so many poor mamas?"

Her response was quick and hard—the back of her hand on my 30-year-old, thought-I-was-grown head. "That's just an excuse to not get me a card," she snapped. "In our poverty-stricken lives things will be bad and good and hard and not so hard, but no matter what, you celebrate who gave you life." She stared ahead, her eyes hard and dark with fury.

My mama passed in 2006 and of course, as always, she was right. She had pushed me to never think inside the krapitalist box us poor people were dealt. No matter how hard it was. And for that and so much more I owed every breath of my being to her and had no business tripping off that damn card.

I prayed and cried for mama. And in my grief and while at the altar, I realized so clearly, and I'm sure with her whispers from the other side, that POOR Magazine needed to move a different way to realize the dream of Homefulness. Like Mama used to say, "It's not people's fault they believe the fucked up lies they were taught about wealth-hoarding and land-stealing." That we needed to teach them another way to live, to give wealth-hoarders and descendants of wealth-hoarders a chance to transform.

But in the end it is up to us poor folks to lift up, to own, to create our Her-Stories and His-stories, to follow our Indigenous life-ways and ancestors teachings. This is our liberation.

I hold this work and the successes of POOR Magazine in a forever traumatized heart crying for my mama, Mama Laure, Mama Gerry Ambrose, Mama Iris Canada, a Black grandmama evicted at 100 years old, and countless incarcerated mamas and Indigenous/migrante mamas killed from the pain of carceral violence, abuse, and the separation from their children and families.

I know Mama was right and this is still no excuse to dismiss Mother's Day. But I still got to call out the hypocrisy of the Happy Day wishes when so many of us mamas are in so much pain.

Krapitalism killed MamaHouse

We were evicted, gentriFUKEd, and burned to the ground out of MamaHouse 1, 2, & 3.

But it was there, in that moment of sorrow and grief, that I had a realization that everything we thought we knew, we did know. I had an epiphany. Homefulness must happen and there would be no more grant dances and philanthro-pimps and trauma porn. That we could not squat land or homes because we poor folks know personally and really what happens when we do. We face arrest. The politricksters and the poLice steal back what was never theirs and come in with guns and tanks like #Moms4Housing and so many more.

Beyond
Dee Allen

Three homes stand
Amidst this lush
Garden so far.
Two in back,
One in front,
Soon to be seven
With four straw bale
Dwellings added to
The liberated land.
A cafe,
A library,
A radio station,

A media centre
Where the destitute,
Evicted, displaced, gentrified out
Can write their own
Tales from their own
Standpoint, reaching digital
Streets, live on wi-fi,
A school to decolonise
Poor children from the
Ways of genocide masters
And re-learn ancestors' knowledge
Thought to be lost to history,
A barnyard with livestock
Supplying families' needs,
Milk & cheese from goats,
Eggs from chickens.
None of these
Are utopian dreams.
They're what this

Lush garden produces everyday,
Aside from vegetables & vines
Scaling up the chainlink steel fence.
All of these
Began with a dream.
Somewhere in 1990s Oakland,
A self-determination
Vision was discussed between
Mother and daughter inside
A parked car they
Both slept in.

Their ambition
Was a solution
To extreme poverty.
Their words contained an alternative
To sleeping in cars, owning scraps of lives,
Living nowhere, deemed undesirable to the eyes.
From homelessness
To homefulness.
Flash-forward: 2012.
When the right place was found,
The smothering asphalt
Covering the land
Had to be broken, lifted, hauled away.
The dream had to live
Beyond two homeless females.
The dust had long cleared.
The construction tools, long in storage.
The asphalt, long removed.
The land, long mended, seeded, planted
And flourishing still.
Homefulness means
"Everyone has a home.
Even plants & animals."
It also means
"There's nothing this
One-way system
Can offer us
That we couldn't
Teach, build or farm ourselves."
Each passing day
Each new project

On this land
Are overtures
Movements conducted
From Oakland's,

Deep East,
Long blighted
On purpose, towards lives
Without undue
Hardship, beyond
Just ideas, movements toward
The growing green future
Beyond this lush garden
And the comfortable lie of Capitalism.

Landless Peoples' Movements Across Mama Earth

From POOR Magazine's PeopleSkool (the Roots of Homefulness' Inspiration) to Mama Earth Liberation

Shack Dwellers' Union – Abahlali baseMjondolo

South Africa is an area in Africa that str`uggled with hundreds of years of apartheid—put in place by the Wite Settlers of South Africa. Aparthed is the separation of people by races, and all of the black and POC people were forced to live in slums—many with no running water or trash pick-up or even housing. People were forced for slave wages to survive—and had no rights. This system was finally thrown out in the 90's thanks to the work of revolutionaries—like Winnie Mandela and Nelson Mandela and so many more.

10 years later after apartheid was ended a different kind of apartheid began- which was the separation of the poorest residents of South Africa. Suddenly over 60% of the population were living in poverty (and the rest were all middle and upper class)—and this was all Black and POC people. Now human rights and land was the struggle.

The Abahlali baseMjondolo (Shack Dwellers) Movement began in Durban, South Africa, in early 2005. It is the largest organisation of the militant poor people in post-apartheid South Africa. Its originary event was a road blockade organised from the Kennedy Road settlement in protest at the sale, to a local industrialist, of a piece of nearby land long promised by the local municipal councillor to shack dwellers for housing.

The movement is organized for and by poor people (shack dwellers-people who live in shacks made of cardboard and found lumber and aluminum) whose goals are NOT TO GET RICH but to get secure housing and access to liberated land so they can build their own visions—without the krapitalist domination of rent.

MST – Movimiento sin Tierra

Moviemiento sin tierra (Landless peoples' movement of Brazil)—The MST is one of the world's largest and most successful social movements, redistributing hundreds of thousands of acres of land to the landless, often working as collectives. Their movement works to empower poor and landless/houseless farmers in Brazil as well as works to preserve traditional cultures and develop identities that include "internacionalismo"—the cultivation of global solidarity among working and oppressed people.

Once again, like all of these movements, their goals are to be self-determined poor people with access to land so they can build their own solutions—so they can achieve food security and end hunger and homelessness for each other and the next generations—not with the goal of becoming the "land-owners" but land stewards.

Sogorea Te' Land Trust

Through the practices of rematriation, cultural revitalization, and land restoration, Sogorea Te' calls on native and non-native peoples to heal and transform the legacies of colonization, genocide, and patriarchy and to do the work our ancestors and future generations are calling us to do.

MOVE Africa

The belief system of the MOVE Organization is based on the writings of John Africa known as "The Guidelines." MOVE are deeply committed revolutionaries the way they honor their father and founder John Africa is they chant, "Long Live John Africa!"

The way MOVE contributes to the revolution is they show an alternative way of living and introduce it to the world. They put out a template that other revolutionaries could see and do good things with.

EZLN – ZAPATISTAS

The struggle of the Zapatistas began on January 1, 1994 with the taking of several major cities in Chiapas. This date coincided with the implementation of NAFTA, which the Zapatistas viewed as a death sentence. NAFTA represented an increase in the polarization in wealth and as a result, an increase in poverty. Feeling that peaceful means had failed to rectify 500 years of oppression up to this point, the Zapatistas called on Article 39 of the Mexican constitution, which allows for citizens to change their government as a basis for revolution.

The goals of the Zapatistas are clearly laid out in their Declaration from the Lacandon Jungle. There are eleven points that they call for improvements including work, land, shelter, food, health, education, independence, freedom, democracy, justice, and peace. This declaration is the heart of their movement and expresses their aims for indigenous people, create an independent press, end hunger and malnutrition, end brutal exploitation of indigenous people, municipal self government, of land, economic and cultural autonomy, and equality for women.

All of these demands result from Chiapas being a very rich natural resource for Mexico while the Maya and other indigenous people suffer blinding poverty and exploitation. The Zapatistas do wish to control the Mexican government, rather they wish more than anything to be treated with dignity, fairness, and put on an equal playing field with the mestizos. They want an end to poverty, being second class citizens, and ignorance.

#Moms4Housing

"Moms for Housing is a collective of homeless and marginally housed mothers. Before we found each other, we felt alone in this struggle. But there are thousands of others like us here in Oakland and all across the Bay Area. We are coming together with the ultimate goal of reclaiming housing for the community from speculators and profiteers."

Words & photos courtesy of #Moms4Housing

Occupy Was Never 4 Me (1 Yr Later)

Tiny Gray-Garcia

September 16, 2012

> *I am the .00025—the smallest number u can think of in yer*
> *   mind—*
> *Didn't even make it to the 99—*
> *love to all of yer awakeninig consciousnessness—*
> *but try to walk in mine…*
>
> *excerpt from "I am 000.25" by Tiny/Po' Poets 2011*

Occupy was never for me. I'm Poor, I'm a mother, I'm disabled, I'm homeless, I'm indigenous, I am on welfare, I never graduated from a formal institution of learning, I have never had a house to be foreclosed on, I am a recycler, panhandler, I am broken, I am humble, I have been po'lice profiled and my mind is occupied with broken teeth, and a broken me. And I am a revolutionary who has fought everyday to decolonize this already occupied indigenous land of Turtle Island in Amerikkka.

I'm not hating. I am glad, like I said when it all first got started, that thousands more people got conscious. I am glad that folks woke up and began to get active. What I am not glad about is that in that waking up there was a weird tunnel vision by so many "occupiers" of the multiple struggles, revolutions, pain and deep struggle of so many who came before you, upon whose shoulders and already "occupied" native lands you are standing on. This is what I have now come to realize is a strange form of political gentrification.

Like any form of gentrification there is a belief by the gentrifiers/colonizers, that their movement is different, new form, that it has little or no historical contextual connection to the ones before it. And that it owes little or nothing to the movements and/or communities already there, creating, struggling, barely making it.

And yes, race, class and educational access matter. I have heard from elders that a similar thing happened in the 60's with the poor people of color movements raging on like Black panthers and Young

Lords then suddenly the "anti-war movement" sprung up, driven by white middle-class college students and the political climate suddenly got large.

This ironic disconnect was never clearer than the way that houseless people, people with psychological disabilities existing outside, were treated, spoken about, problematized, and "dealt with" in the occupations across the United Snakkkes this last year

"We are very excited because the police agreed to come every night and patrol our "camp" because we have been having so many problems with the 'homeless people' coming into our camp," said an occupier from Atlanta, Georgia.

"It took us awhile to forge a relationship with the police, but now that we did we feel "safe" from all the homeless people who are a problem in our camp," said an occupier in Oklahoma

"We have been able to do so much with Occupy in this town, but we are having a real problem with "security," it's because of the large contingent of homeless people near our camp," Occupier from Wisconsin.

City after city, occupation to occupation, in these so-called conscious and political spaces which were allegedly challenging the use of public space and land use and bank control over our resources and naming the struggle of the 99% versus the %1, were playing out the same dynamics of the increasingly po'liced urban and suburban neighborhoods across the US.

The lie of "security" who it is for, the notion of "illegal" people and how some people are supposed to be here and some are not. Our reliance on police as the only way to ensure our community security and the overt and covert veneer of racism and classism alive and well in every part of this United Snakkkes reared its ugly head in all of these Occupations. In many cases the "occupiers" gentrified the outside locations of the houseless people in these cities. Taking away the "sort of" safe places where houseless people were dwelling outside. And yet no accountability to that was ever even considered by the "occupiers"

Perhaps its because the majority of the "occupiers" were from the police using neighborhoods, and/or currently or recently had those homes and student debt and credit and cars and mortgages and stocks and bonds and jobs. Perhaps its because Occupy was never for me or people like me.

In Oakland and San Francisco, the alleged "bastions" of consciousness there was a slightly different perspective. Many of the houseless people were in fact part of the organizing and then eventually, due to deep class and race differences, were intentionally left out or self-segregated themselves from the main "occupy" groups and began their own revolutions or groups or cliques, or just defeated huddles around the camp.

Several of the large and well-funded non-profit organizations in the Bay Area re-harnessed Occupy into their own agendas and helped to launch some of the huge general strikes and marches to support labor movements, migrant/immigrant struggles, prison abolitionist movements and economic justice.

In the case of the poor, indigenous, im/migrant and indigenous skolaz at POOR Magazine we felt we could perhaps insert some education, herstory and information into this very homogenous, very white, and very ahistorical narrative and to the empirical notion of occupation itself, so we created the *Decolonizers Guide to a Humble Revolution* book and curriculum. With this book and study guide and our poverty scholarship and cultural art we supported other indigenous and conscious peoples of color in Oakland who began to frame this entire movement as Decolonize Oakland, challenging the political gentrifying aspects of Occupy itself.

POOR Magazine in an attempt to harness some of the energy and minds of this time towards the very real issues of poverty and criminalization and racism in the US, created The Poor Peoples Decolonization (Occupation) traveling from both sides of the Bay (Oakland to SF) to the welfare offices where so many of us po' folks get criminalized for the meager crums we sometimes get, public housing where we are on 8-9 year long wait-lists for so-called affordable housing, the po'lice dept where all of us black, brown and po folks get incarcerated, profiled and harassed every day not just when we "occupy" and Immigration, Customs Enforcement where any of us who had to cross these false borders, get increasingly criminalized, hated and incarcerated for just trying to work and support our families.

But in the end a small turn-out showed up for our march, I guess our poor people-led occupations weren't as "sexy" as other 99% issues.

Finally, in Oakland there was a powerful push to re-think the arrogant notion of Occupy" itself on already stolen and occupied native lands and became one of the clearest examples of the hypocritical irony of occupy.

After at least a five hour testimony from indigenous leaders and people of color supporters at a herstoric Oakland General Assembly, to

officially change the name of Occupy Oakland to Decolonize Oakland, with first nations warriors like Corrina Gould and Morning Star, Krea Gomez, artists Jesus Barraza and Melanie Cervantez and so many more powerful peoples of color supporters presenting testifying and reading a beautiful statement on decolonization and occupation, it was still voted on that Oakland, the stolen and occupied territory of Ohlone peoples would remain Occupy Oakland.

So as the "Occupy" people celebrate 1 year of existence, I feel nothing. I am glad that elders are being helped to not lose their homes through foreclosure, but truthfully, that work was already being done by so many of us already on the front line of eviction, tenants rights, and elders advocacy.

So one year after Occupy was launched, while lots of exciting media was generated, massive resources were spent, a great number of people were supposedly politicized and the world started to listen to the concept of the %99, the same number of black, brown, poor, disabled and migrant folks are being incarcerated, policed, and deported in the US. The racist and classist Sit-lie laws, gang injunctions and Stop and Frisk ordinances still rage on and we are still being pushed out of our communities of color by the forces of gentriFUKation and poverty. So, I wonder, how have these political gentrifyers changed things for black and brown and poor people? Not at all, actually, but then again, Occupy was never really for us.

Chapter 2
How We Did It

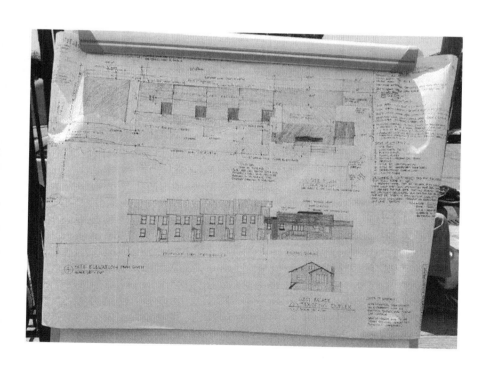

How Did Us Po' Folks Do This?

Tiny, daughter of Dee, mama of Tiburcio

How did us poor, disabled, no-income, and houseless people get the money to "Buy" Mama Earth so we could UnSell her?

Our disabled, criminalized, Black, Brown, Indigenous and mothering bodies are never safe. We are never permanently housed or housing secure or as I say *Homeful* in these occupied streets. No matter how many non-profiteer Devil-oped (never) Affordable housing projects the politricksters claim they're gonna build.

This endless and very real struggle is a constant and ongoing War ON the poor in the form of "Sweeps" and "Clean-ups" and all the other hygienic metaphors used to describe our unHoused, GentriFUked bodies. And it is why we at POOR Magazine have worked for over 11 years to realize a different way to housing security—a vision we call Homefulness.

It is also why we fight and support and resist in any and all eviction resistances, rent control and scamlord fights, take-backs, LANDBACK, and take-overs of occupied Indigenous, sold, and commodified Mama Earth. We as tenants and houseless, Indigenous/landless peoples are all connected by the violence of a settler colonial system that values "private property" aka stolen occupied Indigenous territory over people.

Homefulness and our strategy to resist the violence of krapitalism is not the only way nor are we claiming it is a perfect way. It is merely our way and was born out of multiple forms of violence on our houseless, landless, Indigenous bodies.

Conversely any poverty skola can tell you that long- and short-term home and land reclamation efforts (sometimes referred to as squats) often put disabled elders and families with children in very dangerous positions.

After the violent and horrific eviction of us mamas from MamaHouse, we houseless and poor peoples in the movement we call POOR Magazine knew that we would never be able to continue as

43

a movement in liberation unless we were able to take back resources and stabilize our evicted, poor, and houseless leaders. We needed to get the boot of "rent" off of our collective necks. These struggles and decisions led us houseless poverty skolaz to commit to the Homefulness model of educating, art-making, Un-touring, buying, Unselling, and working outside/only slightly inside the Settler Colonial lies (laws) of permit gangsterism to the ultimate end of spiritually and legally unSelling/liberating as much of Mama Earth as we could with First Nations prayer, permission, and guidance.

Why don't you get a bankkk loan, apply for a grant, or launch a capital campaign?

One of the many questions/suggestions we got when we were trying to realize the very difficult dream of Homefulness was that we should try to get a government loan because we were/are providing actual affordable housing (aka rent-free) to 100% very low and no-income, houseless, disabled families and elders. But as a poverty skola-led project, one thing we knew for certain was we wanted NOTHING to do with bankkksters, philanthro-pimps, or any "money-raising" extractive kkkampaign for dollars.

Our skin collectively crawled at the mere suggestion of anything to do with bankkks and credit. We all came from the violence of bankkkster theft, eviction, debt, lack of paper, or forced criminality due to our poverty. We were all straddling all kinds of records and jackets and poverty crimes.

Our names would collectively light up ChekSystems at the bankkks and our kkkredit skkkores wouldn't even register. We were refugees of the corner sto ATM and an unwilling contributor to the owners of the extractive check cashing stores that lined every barrio and hood.

We also knew, as revolutionaries, that these industries were there to predate and extract on and from our poor people's bodies, ancestors, and cultures. They were the last place we should voluntarily engage with as a "success model" nor have anything to do with any of them.

We knew first-hand the lies of HUD and NoHopeIV and rejection and redlining and discriminatory housing and bankkking policies. We had emerged barely from that rubble, clear-eyed and done.

We came from false border terrorism, profiling, and backs of poLice cars, reservations, prisons, jails, environmentally racialized areas on all of the wrong side of tracks with intentionally poisoned air and water and lands of origin and alleys and tents and sweeps. We came from everything krapitalism builds on to destroy and attack and extract. We knew so clearly from our ancestors and ourselves that we had to do Homefulness a completely different way. It could have nothing to do with all that was there to destroy us.

PeopleSkool

Right before mymama transitioned, I got my first and only legit krapitalist job at a nonprofit organization. Thanks to the first and only paycheck this poverty skola ever received, it enabled me to get my mama housed and the whole POOR Magazine movement current on our office rent.

Crumbling the Myth of The Gift— Deconstructing Donor Denial & Dismantling The Non-Profit Industrial Complex... One outcome at a Time!.. *Revolutionary Change Session 2009*

Wealth-Hoarders Hiding

It was at this job in the non-profiteer (as I call it) world that I met a conscious wealth-hoarder who listened to my dream and believed there was someone I needed "to meet." As I found much to my horror later on (which continues to be the case), almost EVERY non-profiteer and conscious non-profit across Turtle Island is loaded up with trust-funders and wealth-hoarders hiding behind the multiple lies of the "helping industrial complex." Check the *Poverty Scholarship* textbook, Chapter 6.

That said, this JOB saved my life and I have endless gratitude for them taking in this 6th grade (formerly) edumaketed poverty skola so that I could stabilize my mama and my POOR family. And as my brother, Leroy, says, "Get the paycheck, but don't lose yourself in the JOB. It's just a job."

That said, the work was beautiful and complicated and full of good people doing their best to activate change, like most non-profits are. But the krapitalist system in place is intentionally broken and all working very well together to keep poor/Indigenous peoples silenced and outside and profited off of. Non-profiteers are a crucial cog in that wheel.

POOR Magazine's first herstoric meeting with the conscious human, with race and class privilege, was beautiful. Myself, Laure McElroy, Tony Robles, and Leroy Moore explained the vision and work of POOR Magazine and the vision of Homefulness. And unlike EVER, this badass human whose name is Roan said, "This sounds powerFULL. We can do this."

Revolutionary Change—The end of Philanthro-pimps

After six months of Poverty Scholarship curriculum consisting of theatre, story, prayer, poetry, song, love, and trauma, us poverty skolaz built/created/manifested a 3-day intensive seminar un-packed, through art. An akademik from the past might've referred to it as Popular Education, but as this poverty skolaz says, "The population Brings this Popular education." It is also rooted in pan-Indigenous consciousness, multi-nationed prayer and art, and a community art called "talk-story."

Again, all the curriculum, ideas, and "Love-lessons" are internal to poverty skolaz and are outlined in the *Poverty Scholarship* textbook. They are not as simple as "workshops" or teaching in a linear, non-profiteer or akademik model. But rather culled from the herstory of our own internal struggles with trauma, incarceration, criminalization, ableism, homelessness, government crumbs, border terrorism, racism, profiling, poLice brutality. They are all held and lifted up in a deep, long, loving, care-giving, teaching, holding, and dreaming process of PeopleSkool for Poverty Skolaz.

> *The population brings the popular education.*

From the herstoric Revolutionary Change Session, the Solidarity Family of POOR Magazine was born. Young peoples with different forms of race, class, and formal education privilege who have been lied to for centuries about their inherent right to steal, exploit, use, and talk about everything that was and has never been theirs to take. People, who have inherited blood-stained dollars from their ancestors and parents' exploitation work, learn that this doesn't make them privileged to know what to do with it or to even distribute it.

The Solidarity family is a powerFULL force of their own right. They have humbly used the teachings of poverty skolaz and begun a process of un-hoarding, un-colonizing, and ungentriFUKing their own lives and communities so they can take leadership, scholarship, Sister-Ship, and love-ship from poor peoples.

When this #PovertySkola calls people #WealthHoarders & #LandStealers they r simply stating a fact, judgement-free...

pls don't take it person-alleee

we have all been lied to about hoarding being a "success model" and MamaEarth being a Komoditeee... From the poem Truth, medicine for settlers wit privilege

100,000 blood-stained dollars to liberate Mama Earth

The solidarity family raised $100,000 from the Revolutionary Change Session and went on to work closely with poverty and Indigenous skolaz at POOR Magazine to infiltrate other seen and unseen points of access.

From Lawyers to akademiks, I am always teaching these communities to root their decolonization and degentriFUKation work in their own healing, to mend and re-make intentionally destroyed relationships. I teach them to re-meet their own Herstories and histories, their own mamas, grandmamaz, ancestors, cultures, and all the things krapitalism has intentionally stolen from them They have powerful and important healing work to do to help other folks like themselves unlearn and unpack their privilege and generations of hoarded, stolen land, and culture

We got the "check" on the angelVersary of my Mama Dee's passing, March 10, 2010. I knew there were no coincidences there. Mama was working from the other side. Hard.

Gifting, Donating, or "Using" Stolen Land for the 'poor people'

Another move that is welcomed is the "gifting" or offering of land use of so-called privately "owned" Mama Earth by good-hearted wealth-hoarders or descendants of wealth-hoarders/land-stealers. This offering can also come from the so-called "public" (which is actually only for certain members of the raced and classed amerikkklan public) by politricksters in your colonial town or city.

This is a process that is happening with some First Nations communities across Turtle Island thanks to the tireless work by warriors like the Sogorea Te' Land Trust, The Wyot Nation, some return BlackLand initiatives, and other communities in solidarity. It is usually framed as "Repatriation" or as Corrina Gould from Sogorea Te' Land Trust coined it, "Rematriation of Mama Earth." It is all extremely powerful and necessary. Our call as all nations poverty skolaz is that all of stolen Turtle Island should be rematriated to First Nations peoples of this land and enslaved and stolen from Black and Brown peoples.

That said, it is our humble call that Houseless peoples (in collaboration or with permission, protocol, and guidance of First Nations peoples of that land) also be given/granted so-called (never) public land by poltricksters and/or "privately owned" vacant land.

Poverty Scholarship-informed teaching is pleased to create a "use agreement" or Memorandum of Understanding (MOU). Oftentimes

the so-called "land-owners" and/or politricksters get tired, bored, CONfused, and/or greedy and/or "move onto more 'exciting,' 'helping' projects." Other times, their family trust sells the land right under the original person who brokered the plan. Then, the occupied land with houseless people on it often becomes heavily poLiced and politricked, furthering the stealing, evicting, poLicing, and harassing of houseless peoples.

POOR Magazine can help you broker an agreement or MOU or move in this direction if you are unable to find a revolutionary lawyer, contract person who can help you. These projects also need the work/help/model of Elephant Councils and Peoples Agreements of Homefulness. So, if you are interested, we can share all of that as well.

Opening "Branches" of the Bank of ComeUnity Reparations in your stolen towns and cities

We ask every amerikkklan city or town who reaches out to us that you contact the non-profiteers, helping industries, and any volunteers, or "nice" people who are helping you. As houseless folks, we also encourage anyone who may be reading these words right now, to come to the next session of PeopleSkool and follow-up sessions. This way, you can work in solidarity with poor, houseless, and Indigenous peoples to activate these kinds of poor people-led solutions.

Following PeopleSkool sessions, we work closely with each community to help set up a "Branch" of this powerful redistribution model we call Bank of ComeUnity Reparations. This "Branch" supports you and your families, communities, and friends in this liberation of Blood-stained Dollars into Love-stained dollars. Please reach out.

How did we "Get the land": FUKclosure Free and other lies of RealEsnakkes

Once we Po and houseless folks got that "money" we began the insanely violent process of "looking" at "stolen land" as future sites for Homefulness. Our skin began to collectively crawl with CONfusion and gripping fear. So filled with generations of ancestors and elders lies about land and "ownership," we already knew the settler lies (Laws) were set up to hurt everyone they touched. We knew that we couldn't replicate some of the HypoKrazy of so many so-called non-profiteer housing devil-opers. Violence like evicting people to house people and/or getting "cheap" stolen homes at the realE-Snakkke auctions that are oddly reminiscent of all the historical violent auctions of enslaved and Indigenous people's bodies and lives.

Eventually we realized we had to acquire a realtor/broker. These people who are paid to buy, sell, steal, and promote the settler lie of "private property," have heavily commodified insider intel on stolen land, prices, paper trails, and back-stories. You really do need this intel just to navigate through the violent industry of buying and selling, pimping, and playing Mama Earth. This is not to become it or them, but to liberate Mama Earth with all the tools you actually need.

The dichotomy is that most people you encounter in that world don't believe in any version of liberation and unSelling Mama Earth. So, attaining such a person with at least some empathy or even old skool sympathy/charity crumbs in their heart is actually somewhat of a struggle. But as the old krapitalist saying goes, "Money Talks."

Infiltration is Access—Acquiring a Revolutionary Lawyer

Money isn't the only access point that rich people have. It's all the unseen things like akademik connections, good credit, co-signers, no "criminal record," or bad check history, skin privilege (if they r wite), friends in almost every wealth-hoarder industry like law, politricks, real eSnakkke speculation, devil-opment, architecture, bankkking, investing, medicine, engineering, tech, and more.

In the frustrating journey to find a "realtor," my mama was helping again. Her fierce ancestor warrior spirit was working from the other side of the spirit journey. Along with one of the conscious wealth-hoarders with aforementioned skin, akademik, family connection privilege in POOR's solidarity family, Mama found us one.

A call from a solidarity family member to one of their (not as conscious) parents or relatives who then called their friends in the "Real eSnakkke Industrial Complex" accessed a realtor that actually "knew" me and my mama when we were houseless on the street selling art without a license, criminalized every day for our micro-business. This now realtor, whose previous "profession" was a City License poLice person, stopped us multiple times from selling our art because we didn't have a license, leading to the furtherance of our destitute poverty and incarceration throughout our life.

"I've changed," she proclaimed multiple times to me and proceeded to navigate us through the multi-layered, sick, and violent world of buying and selling Mama Earth.

Poisoning, intentional blighting and desecrating Mama Earth.

The other very real issue that happens in all the intentionally blighted poor people neighborhoods, towns, and barrios is the poisoning of Mama Earth. Just like devil-oping and desecrating First Nations ancestors' bones and building of plantation kages, there are gas stations, power plants, run-offs, chemical dumps, and more evil happening everywhere where they think no one is looking or no one cares, aka our neighborhoods. This is very important as you "search" possible

sites and/or accept "donations" of Mama Earth, because sadly so much of her has been destroyed.

That said, there are many organic and amazing decolonial options to "cleaning" and rematriating restoration rooted in Indigenous science that people can work on, embark on, or do. But if you are "buying" to unSell, then you must do what's called an EIR (Environmental Impact Report) for many counties now. However, many don't require it. So, our suggestion is for you to reach out to the local college or university geography, science, biology, or earth sciences department to ask them if someone can come out and help you test the soil. This way, you can find out what you're working with and figure out what's possible as far as making it safe. Or depending on the results, maybe not doing anything with it or on it.

Most of the time, us poor people just live with things like mold, poison, chemicals, and radiation because where else are we going to go? My lungs are permanently damaged from the smog and chemicals of oil drilling and the environmental racism and classism of our poor people neighborhoods where me and mama slept and rented apartments when I was a houseless and low-income child in L.A. Also, this poverty skola was poisoned by mold as an adult living in substandard poor people housing.

These are very hard issues but very real.

Buy that Ugly House and other lies of Krapitalist theft of Mama Earth

In the long racist, wite supremacist trajectory of land theft, colonization, gentriFUKation, genocide, red-lining, eviction, and krapitalism, poor peoples of color and Indigenous peoples are intentionally left out of all the knowledge of land theft and commodification. This is so we can continue to be intimidated and/or bedazzled by violent paper trails and the multiple myths of "success" as it equates to hoarding, accumulation, and feeding on fellow poor people as a success model. Meaning, the endless stream of real eSnakkke seminars on "buying fixer uppers" and "auctions" and tax liens and FUKclosure sales and "short sales" and so on.

All this intentional shutting out adds to us poor people mythologizing an industry which is evil and violent but really not that complicated.

In the very difficult process, POOR Magazine family all decided we needed to teach ourselves more of this knowledge that had been kept from us. Which we did, but then at the end of it realized it wasn't "all that." What's complicated is the intangible shit that you can't learn about, like how some people have generations of stolen land wealth and intentionally keep it to themselves so they can keep us all out. Also, so they can keep us poor people unstable, moving, threatened, and victimized by their so-called ownership. Equity, wealth, capital, savings, and security are all myths of krapitalist settler hoarding/scarcity model ekkkonomy. They aren't real, valid, good, or safe. They are violent and rooted in fear and hate and self-centered-ness.

It's an ongoing conversation in working class and poor communities that as long we get our "own" we will be ok. But actually we won't. Wite Krapitalism sadly isn't that different from POC/Indigneous krapitalism. Yes, it evens out the inevitable "playing field" and enables a certain amount of relaxation and ebbing of fear and PTSD. But as

beautifully outlined in Jared Balls book, The Myth of Black Buying Power, capitalism itself is the root of the problem. And as I would add, it doesn't matter what color the Krapitol it is.

From the settler Lie of discovery to the settler lie of private
     proper-teee
To amerikkklan scarcity models causing us all to be
     Pov-ver-tee—

Everything is a lie when trying to shield the
cult of hoarding, land stealing and I got MINES

This is the church
in the stolen land of I , I , & I

So when Im talking bout liberation, reclaiming and Mama
Earth taking back—we aint speaking bout—re-oppressing mama
earth—with more ownership Smack—

Thats what got us here in the First F-in place—

melanated peoples believing the lie that ownership means you safe- indigenous peoples believing the lie that ownership means we liberate- homeless peoples believing that- ownership means we homeful

IF we don't want to re-oppress, reEvict re-desecrate our communities, our ancestors and Mama Earth—lets actually walk a different way

that has no roots in the colonizers sway

So later in our journey (present day), we are working hard to spiritually and legally UnSell and UnSettle as much of Mama Earth as we can. We follow and listen to First Peoples of this land, who have never bought or sold or pimped or played Mama Earth and who have been her stewards since time immemorial.

In addition to what we are doing in occupied Huchuin, we also try to share this medicine as far and wide as we can through the *Stolen Land/Hoarded Resources Un-Tours Across Occupied Turtle Island (see story on these later in this chapter)*

In addition, it is our goal as poor, disabled, unemployed, and under-employed poverty skolas to actually move 95% off the blood-stained dollar economy and onto a self-sustainable, bartering economy like our many multi-nationed ancestors. But we just aren't there yet. Why not 100%? Because krapitalism has to get a little skin off you or they will actively destroy you. It's reality based self-preservation.

Homefulness on Mixed Use or Commercial Zoned Mama Earth

We were guided through a hellish tour of Unreal Esnakked homes and intentionally, violently blighted Bay Area neighborhoods. Coincidentally, these areas were where all of us poverty skolaz lived or used to live, were gentriFUKEd out of, or were currently sleeping houselessly in.

We were at the point of giving up. We had one of our Elephant Council decision-making meetings with elders and spiritual guides and realized we could Never participate in the ongoing theft of peoples homes and lives (foreclosure, tax liens, evictions). We had to find parts of Mama Earth not currently inhabited at all. This limited our "search" to empty commercial or mixed use land, or long abandoned homes and land.

We chose the mixed use zoned land because commercial "property" sometimes has a little less hater-ation than a so-called "residential neighborhood." We did this because we realized that we would also be dealing with a whole other danger of (all) people's inherent hate/mistrust of poor and houseless people's movements. We held the (unglamourized truth) of fellow povertyskolaz and revolutionaries MOVEAfrica who were bombed by the Black mayor of Occupied Lenape territory, aka Philly, for many more reasons than many people re-tell. These reasons included, the fact that they didn't get down with kkkolonial education of their children, didn't Fuk with corpRape trash "services" and were composting before it was hippie-Sexy, and were practicing grassroots, self-determination tactics wayyy before anyone else even understood them. In addition, the "neighbors" in their Black neighborhood didn't actually support them and oftentimes were calling the city complaining about them.

"I think this is it, the location for Homefulness." One day one of our mentees texted us. They had been helping deal with the realEsnakkke struggle cuz it was way too triggering and time CONsuming for us poverty skolaz to keep "searching" for stolen Mama Earth. Plus we all had other jobs and survival hustles that kept us constantly occupied. No one at POOR Magazine was paid to do this work of land liberation.

When I saw the location my breath was taken away. I began crying and couldn't stop for hours. This was in fact, it. And Mama had everything to do with this. I didn't even really look further than the google map image. I knew.

Herstoric Elephant Meeting

We launched with prayer (as we always do) in the herstoric ComeUnity Newsroom space of POOR Magazine's shared office with the good people of the Living Wage Coalition in San Francisco. We held a huge elephant council of poverty, Indigenous elders, youth, and families to share their ancestors prayers and take part in this herstoric vote to finalize the decision of "Buying" this small part of MamaEarth at 8032 MacArthur (what we would later re-name BlackArthur as named by grassroots, poor people from the BlackRiders movement.

The vote was unanimous. We were commanded by our elders. Go forward and Manifest this Her-Story (I have re-named this word MamaFest).

The papers, all 185 of them, with terrifying names like GRANT DEEDS and Proof of SALE and so many more were signed and re-signed and notarized and passed between so many people involved in the UnRealeSnakkke industry.

The sale was finalized on my mama's bornday (shared, not incidentally with Malcolm X, Yuri Kochiyama, Ho Chi Min and QueennandiXSheba from POOR Magazine).

The Crack-Heads and the Homeless People

"We Po folks riding dirty as usual," sisStar QueennandiXSheba from POOR Magazine announced. The day we went to "see" the land, at least 20 of us poverty skolaz piled into the broke down POOR Magazine Revolutionary Service Van. Our movement had this van as part of our ongoing love-work so we could help our babies and disabled youth and elders all get to and from POOR Magazine/Family Project and Poor Press classes and workshops and all the other multitude of things we inter-dependently work on and support each other with.

Actually, this was only a small slice of the huge multi-generational, multi-cultural village that comprises POOR Magazine.

"He is calling the poLice on us, what do we do??" On the way over the Oakland Bay Bridge from Frisco to Oakland, we got a call from one of our family members who had arrived before us to Homefulness. The ultimate challenge to a grassroots revolutionary movement committed to Never Calling the PoLice is when haters call the PoLice on Us.

"Don't do anything, we are on the way," we told our family.

When we arrived on BlackArthur on that herstoric day in 2011 (not sure what day it actually was), the scamlord from next door was waiting for us.

"You can't do this," said a tall Black man in his late 50's. He was dressed in a polo shirt and Banana Republic tan pants. He waved his hand in the direction of Homefulness while speaking to a couple of POOR families from our group in an over-loud tone. It was so bizarre, but not any different from anything we were used to dealing with all the time. It was just coming from a direction we absolutely didn't expect.

"I thought we had rights." "How can he say this?" We all said in tandem to ourselves, feeling all kinds of triggered fear and terror. As Black, Brown, Houseless, poor, disabled, and profiled youth and families, we all knew what the poLice meant and we were fully ready to be dragged away, harassed, arrested, and possibly shot.

The PoLice arrived and sidled up the land, almost in slow motion. Everything slowed down like a bizarre scene in a horror movie leading to the terrifying culmination.

"Show the PoLice your GRANT DEED," said one of the solidarity family members who was with us.

We all looked at each other, somewhat befuddled. What and Where was the GRANT DEED??? Again, I must repeat, we poverty skolaz are ALL organizationally challenged and all of these blood-stained paper trails were intimidating, triggering and CONfusing. Had it not been for our volunteer admin team who was helping us keep this paper-ish in order we could not have made this happen. The Admin team is comprised of un-paid privileged alumni from PeopleSkool and paid Indigenous, youth poverty skolas who haven't necessarily been through the deep trauma of some of us mamas, aunties, and daughters, brothers and uncles. So, they have the capacity to hold some of this difficult, intimidating paper knowledge.

The grant deed (all 86 pages of it) was found and slowly, nervously presented to the poLice.

TIme passed like a dream. The two kkkops stood there, locked and loaded up with multiple guns, batons, tasers, and shoulder radios. This was artillery meant, purchased, and acquired to kill Black and

Brown and Houseless people. They turned every single page of the GRANT DEED slowly, methodically until they got to the 86th page.

"Ok, looks good. Just continue what you are doing." Just like that, with no more words, handed us the 86 pages and turned around and walked off the sacred land called Homefulness.

We all collectively collapsed. "What Just Happened?" We all said, in tandem. Our privileged mentees had been going about their business, not shocked by any of this. Used to paper privilege and access, it was just another day in raced and classed amerikkklan where private property trumps EVERY-FUKING-THING.

It would be many weeks before any of us poverty skolaz truly overstood spiritually and emotionally what we had just experienced. We taught on this access ALL the time, but for it to happen in real time. To not be shot, harassed, disbelieved, hated, or at the very least disrespected just because of those 86 pieces of paper was absolutely bizarre for us.

The hater neighbor continued to hate. Over the years, he has called us in for non-existent blight notices and sent people to harass us. He tries to cede hate for people doing nothing but bringing love. He openly mocks us, calls us names. The funny tragedy is his "tenants" all loved, collaborated with, and appreciated us. They are us—Black and Indigenous poor people and have been members, supporters, and recipients of all of our love-work. They turned to us for jailhouse lawyering when the scamlord was harassing, hating and unjustly evicting them. And of course we did everything we could to help, stand with them, and facilitate justice for them like we do for all of us poverty skolaz.

As my mama used to say if someone treats you like shit, they are probably treating a lot of other people the same way. And yes the Scamlord next door is not only a bad neighbor (he lives off-site in a very bugie, wealth-hoarding neighborhood) but a bad Scamlord. And sadly most of them are.

How Do you Figure out Who Lives in Homefulness

Once we knew we were going to MamaFest Homefulness. We multi-nationed, multi-racial, multi-lingual and all generations of poor, disabled,
houseless, Indigenous cultural workers, media producers, Herstory-
writers and prayer-carrying mamas, fathers, daughters, suns, uncles,
elders, and youth began a two year-long process internally at POOR
Magazine of "writing" the **Manifesto for Change** and the **Declaration
of Inter-Dependence**. These are two sacred internal agreements that
we made with each other in a long series of meetings of what we call
The Elephant Council.

As a multi-nationed, pan-Indigenous, multi-generational, poor,
Black, Brown, and houseless people-led movement, we follow the
teachings of our ancestors from all four corners of Mama Earth. We
practice eldership, prayer, and ancestor honoring beginning with the
first peoples of this occupied land.

We use the multiple circles, councils, and eldership structure to
decide together who we are that builds and lives and works together.
We use these to solve the multitude and very serious issues that all

of us traumatized, colonized, in struggle peoples deal with everyday, including violence to each other, abuse, PTSD, trauma, and so much more.

We do this Indigenous restorative justice model and love-model as a healing practice and a real practice so we NEVER engage with the State or any of its armed agents or kkkorts. This is VERY hard and one of the many teachings we share with fellow communities. (Refer to the How to Not Call PoLice Handbook, and workshop series, available on poorpress.net or for free for any poverty skolaz who want a copy)

What's important for the building of any version of Homefulness specifically is the overstanding of who your community is. In other words, who is going to live there.

The treatment from the ScamLord next door wasn't new. Poltricksters, Anti-social workers, and hater neighbors have always referred to us with the racist, classist label "the homeless people" (or bums, hobos, crack-heads, and more.) But our lack of access to a roof does not define us. In fact we are a multi-verse, just like any community or person. We just don't happen to have access to enough blood-stained dollars or connections to keep a roof over our heads.

MamaFestation and all the ways we hold each other in interdependence

That said, the protection of children, elders, mamaz, disabled peoples, and all vulnerable people is one of our top priorities in POOR Magazine. Homefulness is NOT a Hippie idea and everyone can't "just live together" and somehow be ok. Each community needs to decide who they "are," who is in the most need, and who is committed for the heavy lift of building, "MamaFesting" as I call it, a different way to be in community. It is a different way that isn't a "cult" or a non-profiteer program held together with an EXECUTIVE DIRECTOR, pulling literally thousands of dollars from the "helping" industry to "help us" poor people. It is not the Jeffersonian and the for-profit model of a BOARD of DIRECTORS with its series of settler colonial tax codes, threats of PoLice, and mandated reporting.

Homefulness and POOR Magazine's principles are informed by *Poverty Scholarship: Poor People-led Theory, Art, Words and Tears Across Mama Earth*, the companion text to this handbook.

Rather POOR Magazine, over a series of 25 years of our collective life as a movement, has established a series of Poverty Scholarship-informed principles which are very rooted in deep and transparent realNESS, truth, and accountability. They are not informed by shame.

As poverty skolaz who have survived (barely) different forms of physical, personal, and State sponsored abuse and incarceration, we know that our shared survival and MamaFestation of poor people-led interdependence requires a completely different set of upfront commitments to absolute honesty, long-term healing, and love. We practice respect first and hold each other to it.

We also know truly and deeply the struggles we have seen and the harm to each other we are capable of. We know, as informed by ongoing prayer, healing, and check-in and love sessions what is necessary to keep each other safe. Most of the time this is very hard and means that everyone can't live in the same community. It means that race and class and racism and classism, abuse, violence, aggression, patriarchy, trauma, substance use, and disability of all kinds, seen and unseen, must be dealt with, addressed, and talked out. It means people with race, class, and formal education privilege have no inherent right to space, place, or decision-making ability or power over others. This horizontal organizing is key at all times. Everyone has a voice. Elders hold sacred space as elders (not only rooted in age or generation but in time along with organization, work, and trust). It means elders, youth, and other communities must receive more help than others, that spaces must be held open for some communities and not others, and these decisions must be established with love and time.

We created these principles over many years but with the matriarchal, Indigenous leadership of my fiercely real OG poverty skola, torture survivor Mama Dee. We were very clear about all of this before there was ever a conversation about creating a community living space.

In these sacred documents and agreements, we made conscious decisions to follow POOR Magazine's priorities of housing/love-working and supporting children and elders. This meant that, for instance, no one who had any history/herstory of sexual abuse of youth or children could reside at Homefulness.

We then set about creating the living documents known as the People's Agreements. These documents clearly outlined the Rules of Respect (see an example on page 24) agreements to not harm each other, to be sober in public spaces, and the protocols for handling acts of aggression and harm. These are living agreements and are constantly changing as the issue of violence and substance use are MAJOR and continue to be vexing and hard. It is hard to never engage with the state when we have all been colonized that way and to hold each other close enough, but not too close to ensure we have space but also healing.

This changes with each person that comes into the ComeUnity and varies with each community. (This poverty skola can come to ComeUnities and work with your encampment, group, or nation to help you through this very complex, prayerful, and powerful process).

That said, once you decide who your community of residents most in desperate need is, you also have to make the hard choices that some of your folks won't be able to be housed there. For instance, if most of your folks are single adults and/or elders, some of whom have had situations with the State, accusations of abuse of a minor, or are vulnerable people, you must have the hard conversation that that

community is not appropriate for families with children under 18. And the converse is true if your community in most need is families with children, then that is not a place for single adults.

We completely overstand that the STATE is full of racist and classist snares to wrongly and unjustly accuse people of all kinds of things they never did. This is also true for the way even peer to peer or intimate relationship violence can be weighted in the direction of racist and classist judgement patterns. And holding ALL of that, protecting people without poLice means an ongoing process of talking, thinking, accountability, and love. It is NOT at all easy.

Please realize in advance this is a commitment to ongoing accountability sessions, re-figuring, and healing. That it isn't a magic bullet or panacea for all. And these are VERY serious issues to grapple with beyond the facile narratives and hashtags thrown around in the Defund the PoLice and Abolition movements. Many of these movements come from privilege and access and have never, as Mama Dee said, missed a meal or faced real danger, real life, or real violence. This is where all the healing and deciding and trauma un-packing, movement building, writing, theatre, and loving circles come in.

Taken Down from the Inside

We bring the following cautionary tale as the Elephant Council and the work of our elders does not ensure this will be easy and without huge obstacles. Oftentimes no matter how hard you work to move, different trauma and colonization are also real and have destroyed so many of us already. This will be a very real part of your movement's struggles and work.

Suffice it to say, we had a member who was relatively new in our circle who looked like us, talked like us, and claimed to have exactly the same values. But as soon as they "moved in" to Homefulness, they seemed dead set on destroying us.

After a barrage of lies and social media attacks, violence against us and targeting/using our children and their own, they claimed, "I'm not going anywhere." They proceeded to refuse to move, plan to move, or accept any mediation or long-term plan of stepping away.

We offered to raise reparations, find them a new place,and find a compromise. Instead, the lies and hate just continued to flow. It was leveled at all of us in the organization even though we had done nothing but support this person and love and welcome them.

The heart-wrenching, traumatizing struggle spanned 1 ½ years of Elephant Councils. The person refused to attend meetings or accept the collective votes of the Family Elders Circles and Elephant Council to step away, even though we even offered massive support. It finally culminated in them leaving, and continuing the smear campaign wherever and with whomever they encountered. The entire time they were there they continued to attack us and never supported us. They never worked within the community or contributed to any of our work.

The crucial part of this internal violence is what we learned and what we would cautiously share with you in this handbook and to our future seven generations of liberators and revolutionaries. Only being politically or even emotionally aligned with someone does NOT mean they will be someone you can collectively live with. Sometimes people's trauma and baggage are so dangerous and volatile that you can never work/live in collaboration.

To this end, the People's Agreement would change again with the addition of another agreement that we would make to each other. We realized we needed to raise ComeUnity Reparations to cover rent on a prospective resident's current place no matter how bad it was. It might be for a motel or parking space (if the future resident was unhoused). So, if someone moved here from some other place or from a tent or "safe parking space," then it was crucial they try Homefulness out for 6 months before they made a life-long commitment to it. If, like us, you commit to Never evicting anyone or resorting to engaging with the poLice, you have to figure out where they can go if it doesn't work out. UnSelling MamaEarth means Forever Homes

One of the many crucial aspects of MamaFesting Homefulness is once you unSettle and UnSell Mama Earth and its no longer a commodity to buy and sell and pimp and play, the threat that every poor person and family feels about eventual displacement or rent theft or rent hikes or tax hikes or imminent domains or gentriFUKation/removal changes.

In fact, what it means is everyone who moves/lives at Homefulness has secure housing for life. And not just for them but for their children and their children's children and beyond.

The real struggle, as we found out, is the settler Kolonial Lies (laws) in place that we have to grapple with that actually protect/provide/enable the buying and selling pimping and playing. In actuality, our work is to create a new designation in the "law" that ensures that Homefulness on Mama Earth can actually stay free.

As I outlined in the story, *Trust in What???- the Settler Lie of Land Trusts*,(find this story later in this chapter) Land Trusts are all we revolutionaries and land liberators and houseless people think we have, but they are not everything. No matter how they are set up, they all have expiration dates. Sometimes it might be 15 years, sometimes 99 years. But ultimately even if your "life" is safe, your babies and grandbabies and generations to come are not "safe" or securely homed. And the same tax codes apply.

Deed Restrictions and Land Liberation

In addition, we also discovered that once you find a conscious lawyer willing to work pro-bono for your movement and/ or one of you are willing to be a jailhouse lawyer like I have had to do (learning in or outside the razor wire plantation walls the laws that incarcerate every poor person they get), there is a long process you need to go through (which we are just beginning) to put a **Deed Restriction** on your "GRANT DEED" so it can never be flipped into a commodity.

How did we Build Homefulness

There are alot of lies we are told and sold about who is an expert, who is qualified to write, speak, teach, and create. This is something we teach and unpack in the Poverty Scholarship textbook and PeopleSKool.

The other thing that's lied about is the notion of who can design, engineer, and build homes. All of these acts of work have been transformed into "professions" by akkkademia, settler colonial lies (laws), politricks because there is a billion dollar industry built on its "pro-fees-alism." This brings us to the idea of who is considered an "architect" and who is considered a laborer, who is considered an agricultural designer/landscaper and who is considered a gardener, and who is considered a contractor and who is considered a worker. The list goes on and on.

One of the many revolutionary liberation moves we have MamaFested at Homefulness is the Revolutionary Building Circle. This is where us houseless people sit with and decide what will be built and where and how and who will partake in these designing and conceptualizing sessions. This is a direct resistance to this proFees-alism.

528 years, 22 years and all of our lives of endless struggle....Poor People built these Homes with a poem- a poem that wound thru shelter beds and tents, poLice sweeps and the lie of rent....

Communities with Street (ac)cred-itation are architects and engineers and lawyers too!!!

At almost the same time we were working on liberating Mama Earth for Homefulness in occupied Huchuin aka Oakland, we were working with First Nations land liberators Corrina Gould, Johnella LaRose, Wounded Knee DeOcampo and many more to take back a sacred

shellmound in so-called Vallejo known as Sogorea Te' Land Trust. This resistance turned into a 109-day occupation which POOR Magazine re-ported and sup-ported on, slept at and lifted up in every way we could.

At the end of the occupation, where the politricksters of that city ended up desecrating that sacred site, I met with Corrina and proposed the idea of Homefulness. I asked if she would be willing to guide us, pray with us, be on our Elephant Council and Mamafest with us houseless peoples from all four corners in her people's land of origin aka Huchuin, Ohlone, Lisjan land.

She said yes and it was one of the most important moves we made in our prayer and MamaFestation journey to liberating Mama Earth.

It is why we urge all landless/homeless people's movements to practice protocol with First Nations peoples of the land they are working to liberate. Reach out with offerings of mutual support and humbly ask for their permission, involvement, and/or blessing.

This isn't necessarily linear or easy or straightforward. Don't expect people to respond to you right away. It is the creation of a long-term relationship.

Architects/Builders/Designers and Engineers with and without Paper Privilege

From Leo Stegman (a revolutionary peoples lawyer) to Muteado Silencio to Mark G to Will to Donald, all builders of life and struggle and houses and poetry and dreams.

It is and was never easy to explain this concept to people in the "building trades" or more importantly the industries of architecture, design, and engineering. So much gratitude to some of the paper-privileged architects, designers, and engineers such as Bob Theis, Joe Igber, Dunya Alwan, and the good folks at *Architecture for Humanity* who although they didn't really understand where we were going, they did try to help us conceive of the idea.

Considering Dunya and Bob, they sat with our building circle for hours, days, weeks, months, and now years seeing the Homefulness vision to the finish line. They leveraged their institutional paper privilege which enabled us to get approval from the Politricksters and Bureaucrats at City Hall.

They did this all pro-bono (with no money upfront or at any point). This was HUGE as we would not have been able to move forward with our dreams without their radical redistribution of paper privilege, time, and resources.

That said, there is aLOT of hetero-patriachal rage in the building trades which is really crazy and hard to hold, and takes a deep effort to navigate and work around. It is NOT a revolutionary space. And sometimes there is nothing you can do about that. MamaFesting means you need to recognize that all spaces and communities have their own protocols and requirements. But also and most importantly, that as poverty skolaz we also have our own knowledge. So, you are coming into a situation with a position of humble power.

In this MamaFesting with settler lies (laws), there is also constant and violent permit gangsterism. The City and private CorpRapeshuns who think they own Mama Earth make gads of blood-stained dollars on the so-called Inspection business. From the Zoning departments to the Building and permits, it is an endless and unbelievably expensive money trail. A garden variety street hustle ain't got nothing on the city politricks from expeditor fees to move your project up in a line to thousands of dollars for a piece of paper that says you can put in plumbing to $15-25,000 for each water meter to tell the "Water gangsters" how much you owe them for Mama Earth's water that they think they own to charging us a several thousand dollar "late fee" for taking too long to build when their costly fees are why we took so long to build.

The CONfusion of Volunteerism

One of the many myths is that we can all be "volunteers." On the contrary, poor people can barely cover our rent and our food, much less work for free.

This notion is promoted or demanded by privileged people who have never missed a meal and racist, classist kkkort systems that are already unjust and even some CONfused non-profiteers. But as my

Mama Dee clearly teaches in the *Poverty Scholarship* textbook, poor people not living on our lands of origin in a krapitalist system that charges us for every step, every bite, every sip of water we take and every roof we shelter under need to be supported in the work we do. We need to be supported even in the work for the so-called community (which ironically is us). So, we as a poor people-led movement completely rebuke that wrong-headed notion and work really hard to raise ComeUnity Reparations to compensate ourselves and fellow poor people for the work we do.

Also, a lot of blab by poltricksters and philanthro-pimps is generated about "Hiring from the Community." But in the end, it usually ends up with more plantation system labor with wealth-hoarding, multi-national CorpRape builders and devil-opers contacting and subCONtracting to the very racist and classist building industry.

On the other hand, POOR Magazine from the beginning of Homefulness has not only resisted the notion of who is a builder and architect in real time but we have consistently supported local poverty skolaz as builders, roofers, plumbers, and electricians. And we have compensated everyone with the highest "living wage" we could raise. This is not easy and we have not been able to raise as much as we believe people are worth. As such, we are currently in the process of moving the structure of all of our collective labor projects to an actual cooperative with the goal of figuring out how we can acquire a group insurance plan like the badass Black-run cooperative Mandela Grocery.

Similarly, Mama Dee clearly stated in her Mamafesto on Race, Class privilege (*Poverty Scholarship* textbook) that folks who hold different forms of race and class privilege should in fact "volunteer" their time in non-colonizing ways, non-gentriFUking ways.

This is NOT the PeaceKkkorps

No we don't need anyone to "save" us poor folks and in fack we ask privileged folks to limit their time and space on the actual land but to help with backend things like bookkeeping and data bases. But more importantly, we ask that they help with organizing, lifting up, and educating their own communities on How To Not Call the PoLice, how

to Not CONTinue the wealth-hoarding and land-stealing, evicting, profiling and anti-poor people hating. Equally important, we know that their own communities of privileged people, including their families and peers, desperately need the healing work of ComeUnity Reparations. This is not so they can opt it and steal it and write about us without us and launch more research studies and thesis projects and cultural anthorWRONGology projects, but so they can listen and learn and bring that healing to their own krapitalist diseased peoples and selves.

And as Mama Dee would say the "sexy" pseudo-savior work of writing, researching, and even "organizing" and protesting "with" us is not what is needed AT ALL. What is needed is radical redistribution of resources and time and energy and blood-stained dollars so we can build our own solutions like Homefulness, EZLN, Poor People's Army, The Self-Help Hunger Program, and Cob on Wood to name a few. Refer to the *Poverty Scholarship* textbook, Chapter 11 for more on these lessons for privileged people.

Poor people sweat equity and the lie of Rent

We don't charge rent at Homefulness. We ask for a contribution to the money we have to pay on taxes, insurance, utilities, and trash services.

We are working on multiple fronts to reduce our involvement with any of these utility CorpRapeshuns to install solar and create a usable series of gray-water and compost systems other than the ones that the City provides. But real talk, no matter how many wite people with dreadlocks who all hyphy come in with Compost and Gray water systems, Everything is work. And these people CONsistently start all big and then walk away over time when it stops being "sexy" aka fun.

So we move in the slow and steady way we are able to as poor people doing our best with what we have and what we can MamaFest. This means we might still be on so many of these Corprape providers for many years to come but we are doing our best.

We are currently fighting for exemption from taxes but it hasn't happened yet. It will only happen because of pro-bono attorneys from Sustainable Economies Law Center, who are helping with this EXTREMELY difficult process. Nut all non-profits doing this kind of project should qualify for exemption from taxes. It's just a struggle, as usual.

Dollar amount is agreed to for contribution by each resident for off-setting (not necessarily Covering) the costs

In a similar way, so-called co-housing, collective/cooperative housing, and even Anarchist housing squats set up so-called sweat equity exchanges for rent. But these are often set up by able-bodied, middle class people who have no concept of what I call Poor People Work or poor people sweat. This was and is a very important part of Poverty Scholarship-informed housing—to unlink our minds from the ableist, ageist notion of what work is. Beginning with Mama Dee's WeSearch (poor people-led research as this poverty skola calls it) for *POOR Magazine Volume 3: The Work Issue.* Here, she looked at multiple forms of unrecognized, criminalized, and unseen poor peoples labor and how those forms of poor people labor are unseen and de-legitmized for profit and exploitation. She also looked at how our honoring of them in terms of "equity" is an act of liberation and poverty scholarship in action. Honoring what we can do, no matter how small or unseen, is what we call Love-work, liberation, theory creation, and more. Check the *Poverty Scholarship* textbook, Chapter 7.

Examples of **Poor People Sweat Equity** are mothering, gardening, recycling, taking care of ancestors' altars, writing poetry, care-giving, sitting with elders, leading healing circles, writing letters, social media stewardship, grocery bagging, prayer, reading to children, watching, stewarding the Poor people's library, and more.

The lie of krapitalist productivity dictates what Work is. These are always rooted in the violent hamster wheels and are never about love or care or spirit.

Similarly, each community makes a decision about what their community's actual costs are and what people's sliding scale contributions will be. In the Homefulness model, there is no "requirement" of monthly contribution because sometimes people can't do anything or contribute anything. They can't lose a side hustle or a money hook-up they had and there is NO PUNITIVE consequence. It is simply explained to the Elephant Council who handles money and more is pulled from the Bank of ComeUnity Reparations for that month's bills.

As stated earlier, we not only engage with poverty skola builders from the community but we also make a decision to pay community poverty skolaz who live on the premises for things they do to keep this going.

For instance, our Deecolonize Academy teachers are paid for their time from whatever we can raise and/or the Homefulness fund as our education projects are integral to our liberation model. That goes for other tasks like radio and video production and help with Sliding Scale Cafe.

By the same token, many of us do not pull any money from the project. It is truly based on what is the need of the community and decided on by the Elephant Council. Dee Allen and I, both of us formerly houseless/displaced residents of Homefulness, work elsewhere on side hustles for income or in my case, receive EBT (food aid) and support from the community full time without ever taking a dime from POOR Magazine. WE don't "pay" ourselves to help ourselves.

And again, our long-term goal is to move mostly off the Blood-Stained dollar ekkkonomy and bring barter-based micro-businesses into the land. This would enable each poverty skola to support their families, elders, and babies and contribute to the costs of Homefulness.

Everything is on a holistic sliding scale and we do believe also that POOR people's scholarship, art, theory, time, and love-work must be supported and legitimized, spoken and taught by us for everyone else.

MamaFesting for MamaEarth

No matter how hard and how crazy all of this has been and continues to be, for the first time in this houseless mamaz life I'm homeful and I wouldn't have done anything different. Ase, Ometeotl Ahoooooo!

In this time of MamaEarth destruction (so-called Climate Change), we poverty skolaz believe there is no other way but for all of us to stop hoarding, stealing, lying, politricking, gentriFUKing, sweeping, cleaning, incarcerating, criminalizing, LieGislating, DEvil-oping, and Taking and begin radically sharing, redistributing, liberating, reparating, praying, visioning, MamaFesting, and interdependently love-working for all of our collective liberation, our ancestors, and MamaEarth. This is nothing new as we learn and listen to our First Nations ancestors and all of our Indigenous ancestors. Mama Earth is Not for Sale and Never Has been. It is way over time to UnSell and UnSettle her and all of us.

....And this povertySkola is always here to help/steward, teach, share with any movement who wants to MamaFest this liberation. Holllla Back!

FAMILY COUNCIL, ELEPHANTS COUNCILS, ELDERS' COUNCILS & ALL The Circles

Tiny Gray-Garcia

In addition to PeopleSkool's poverty journalism, poor press poetry, writing and radio workshops for poverty skolaz and degentriFUKation seminars for folks with Race, Class and Formal Education Privilege, we have several circles at POOR Magazine/Homefulness and Decolonize Academy. This is how we decide all of our decisions, resolve and deal with conflicts, and hold all of us fellow poor people in accountability and love, no matter how hard it gets. All of the below listed circles begin in a good way with all-nations prayer.

The Elephant Council

Elephant Council is so named because, like Elephants, we poor and traumatized folks are interdependently connected to each other. And no matter how hard a white zoologist might work to keep alive in "captivity", an elephant cannot survive without their family. Also like

Elephants, we are matriarchal—Mamas and Daughters, Sisters, Aunties, and Grandmamaz lead our core values while we work with, listen to, respect, and rely heavily on our Uncles and Suns, Fathers and Brothers.

In the Elephant Council, all of us are leaders and this is the ONLY way we decide things. We call our main decision-making body which is led by poverty, disability, and Indigenous skolaz—the elephant circle—as we move like our elephant relatives—interdependently— ALWAYS down to think through and continue to work on and vision this poor and Indigenous peoples-led movement.

ComeUnity Newsroom Circle/ ComeUnity Orientation Meeting

We meet once a month, for the whole ComeUnity to learn, share, create community news, and get support for actions and create their own media and advocacy.

Revolutionary Building Circle

We hold our Revolutionary Building Circle to Deal with all building decisions between "papered" builders, so-called architects, and engineers (who donate their time as part of their ComeUnity Reparations) alongside community Indigenous builders and poverty skola builder-leaders at Homefulness. We deal with the settler colonizer papers, requirements, struggles, and permit gangsters, who we intentionally navigate, so this poor people's movement will never be stolen from us by the multiple settler colonial lies (laws) put in place to steal poor and Indigenous people's land, lives, and equity.

Healing from Addiction thru Art, Liberation and Spirit (HEAALS) Circle

This is an extremely important circle, held every other week to help us trauma-filled poor people who have sought out the man's poison (alcohol, substances) to numb, self-medicate, and survive another day of poverty in amerikkkka. Holding each other through healing and love and hope and change through spirit, art, meditation, and talk-story from all four corners.

Hoarder/Clutterer Trauma Support Circle

This is held bi-weekly for Homefulness residents to deal with our traumatized souls. These are very real ways of coping through collecting.

Family Council for Youth at Deecolonize Academy and Family Council for Adults at POOR Magazine

Similarly, if we have serious breaches of our Rules of Respect, in either our youth/children school community or our adult community, the Elephant Council calls a Family Council. This is another circle of eldership, healing and accountability.

FAMILY ELDERS Council

Our last and ultimate circle is called when things cannot be resolved in the other circles and to make final decisions that are permanent.

These are held as both healing medicine and resolutions to decide where and what we should do as per our peoples' agreement. These can sometimes lead to asking people to permanently or temporarily step away, for long periods of time or forever.

All of our teaching so far brings us to overstand and understand the values and moves of our multi-nationed Indigenous ancestors from all four corners. They have worked in different ways together to solve and resolve each other's problems. They also shouldn't be fetishized, as if they didn't have flaws or nothing to do with this krapitalist, hoarding culture.

Controlled by the wite-hetero-patriarchal cult of independence, the ways in which people are forcibly (read: voluntarily) separated into what I call the separation nation is considered a success. It begins with age/grade separated schools progressing to the cult of angst and then "voluntarily" traveling to cities, towns, and states hundreds and thousands of miles away to age/grade separated schools and colleges. All of which is considered success. The ways that we are encouraged/almost forced to leave culturally and societally away from all of the things that we or our ancestors came from, our collective systems of protection, love and actual security, and our origin stories, ancestors, families, homes, communities. Until we end up struggling with isolation, fear, and alone-ness, make unsafe choices, and have no elders to assist us, school us, and protect us. (Disclaimer: this narrative doesn't apply to people targeted, abused, and tortured by their families. This is some of the de-gentriFUKing and un-colonizing work we do at PeopleSkool presented by POOR Magazine poverty skolaz and some of the many issues we address in the *Poverty Scholarship* textbook.)

These sad realities of colonial domination and krapitalist CONfusion have led us houseless/Indigenous/landless poor peoples in diaspora from all four corners to create several circles of healing, decision-making, accountability, and comeUnity justice at POOR Magazine. The Elephant Council is held in place and dictated by our Rules of Respect. When someone breaks from the rules of respect we also call upon another circle. (see above)

Our Rules of Respect or Peoples Agreements are fluid documents that are subject to change and growth all the time based on the changing, fluctuation of the Homefulness residents, POOR Magazine family, Decolonize Academy student body and other projects' needs. Because again there are macro and micro ways we re-traumatize each other as colonized peoples trying to organize each other and build a different, healing space. What you saw in the vignettes were really obvious ways, but sometimes they're literally much smaller and very internal. So we had to make these very fluid documents from the beginning rooted in love. And that's a very important aspect to any folks who are thinking about some of these models for themselves and their communities. If you make a series of agreements with each other, don't make them static, because things Always change, communities change and crises can change. And as well, you never quite know what triggers people's trauma until you end up with a trigger. So you, again, can have these beautiful sessions where you come up with agreements all day and twice on Sundays, and they may mean nothing in practice.

A complicated example of this is we had a conflict in an Elephant Council where one of our beautiful poverty scholar members literally flipped off and cussed out another member. Which led us to realize that the rules of respect document we were working with was absolutely not comprehensive enough for our new larger family and extended family of houseless and homefulness resident poverty skolas.

Again, it's not a magic bullet and sometimes it means asking someone to step away, with financial and physical support, no kkkort or poLice engagement.

BureauCRAZY

Making it Hard for Poor People to Build Housing

Homefulness Timeline

Just a tiny fraction of the hundreds of insane, Blood-stained dollar-infested, permit gangster struggles we poor people have dealt with just to get us to MamaFest this land liberation.

> **Feb 12, 2012:** Booked jackhammers to remove asphalt covering Homefulness #1

March 28, 2012: Receive a "Notice to Abate" by the City of Oakland

> *Description of the "violation": "A permit to make alterations required under this complaint expired without final approval. The only remaining issue is the lack of a window that meets egress requirements for the lower level of the building.* **Failure to comply will result in substantial fees and penalties.*** "

April 2012–Feb 2013: Ongoing Permit Gangster harassment by the City of Oakland

> *From April 2012-Feb 2013, we received consistent threats of demolition and legal action if we did not complete immediate actions and pay for permits.*

July 2016: Breaking ground on Homefulness

June 2017: Permits completed AND Urgent Ask for $300,000 needed to construct all 4 townhomes at once, as opposed to the initial plan of pouring foundation for all four and completing an initial show house first.

November 2017: Received a recycling compliance hold from Green Halo
> *The warning stated: "THIS PROJECT DOES NOT CURRENTLY meet the minimum recycling standards mandated by the City of Oakland and may be subject to a HOLD on INSPECTIONS AND OR PERMIT SUSPENSION."*

May 2018: Fee harassment from East Bay Municipal Utility District (EMBUD)
> *They had deadlines to receive appropriate/non-inflated charges, but a missed deadline meant being charged at the new, inflated rate. These deadlines be some BULLSHIT, same old story everywhere, it's expensive to be poor and they charge the shit out of you for not having money.*

July 2018: Slapped with $70,000 water meter installation cost estimate.

August 2018: Ongoing EBMUD additional costs harassment
We either had to re-plumb the houseline, which costs money, or they would kill the meter at the water main and charge us $1,739 for it.

April 2019: Liability Insurance is Renewed
The premium for General Liability and Property coverage was raised by $33.

September 2019: Bank of COME-Unity Reparations is launched

January 2020: Building official with the City of Oakland sends a condescending response re: permit extension
They agreed to extend the permit for 30 days, within which time we had to request and pass an inspection. After this the permit would be extended for another 180 days.

January 2020: Emergency Action Needed! PERMIT GANGSTERS HAVE SHUT US DOWN with BULLSHIT

June 2020: Residents survived covid
Had to get Porta Pottie for the Neighborhood and us so we could keep working and keep the school and radio station open—costing us $600.00 per month!!!!

The Struggle to Build Housing when you are Homeless: Poor and Homeless Builders Struggle with Permit Gangsterism and Politricks

03 February 2020
by Lisa "Tiny" Gray-Garcia

"You owe $72,000 for these water and sewer permits," said the East Bay Municipal Utility District (EBMUD) clerk to Homefulness.

"We don't have that kind of money," we said.

"Well maybe you shouldn't be building this project then...," EBMUD replied. And then without waiting for a response, walked away from us. These lines of disgusted discouragement left us, the Homefulness building co-leaders, destroyed. One more little murder of the soul, as my Mama Dee used to call it.

But sadly, this was nothing new. This latest demand just took the permit gangsterism (as I called it) to a new high.

Just to begin building this landless/houseless peoples solution to homelessness, we were asked to come up with $29,000. More money than most of us had ever seen. And then there were the individual and constant building permits. Permit after permit was demanded and each one had its own exorbitant price and its own expensive inspection attached to it, which ran $200-500 depending on the agency, the utility, and/or the fee. For example a permit was required for toilets. Just for the paper that said we could do it, not the appliances, the plumbing, or the sewer or the water itself was priced at over $8,000. It took hours and days and weeks and months and years of teaching folks with race and class privilege about radical redistribution of hoarded and stolen wealth to poor and Indigenous people, which is how we fund this land liberation work. It also took years and days and months of planning, working, organizing, praying, dreaming, poem-bringing, theatre-creating, story-telling, protesting, marching, and teaching. Finally in 2011, us poor, migrant, Indigenous, and homeless builders stood shoulder to shoulder with an architect, designer, and engineer and other folks with different forms of race, class, and formal education privilege (who had those papers saying they were "qualified" builders and engineers), we submitted this prayerful and powerful project to the City of Oakland.

From the trauma of our own broken lives as evicted, houseless, and gentriFUKed people trying to manifest something different together on this stolen land to the trauma we get when we try to resist the set-up from the get-up, these kinds of statements were said more times than I actually want to remember. From poltricksters to permit gangsters, public and private, there has been an ongoing refrain of how hard, how expensive, how impossible, and ultimately how unrealistic it is for us homeless and poor people to build our own solution to home-lessness we call Homefulness. But we pushed on. We refused to give up to these settler-colonial lies (laws) and sanctioned thieves of Mama Earths' water, energy, minerals and earth.

But the paper trails are covered in blood and always have been since the Stealing Fathers (Founding Fathers) claimed that Mama Earth and all her peoples were something to buy and sell. They committed genocidal terror on the Indigenous peoples of this land and then enslaved, exported, and perpetrated more genocide on more African and Turtle Island Indigenous peoples to manifest it.

Now the genocide, removal, and colonization looks like blight notices, bankkksters, evictions, poLice, mortgages, permits, imminent domain, devil-Opment, and seminars on how to Buy Your Ugly House.

"The 'City' of Oakland has been charging us several thousands of dollars we didn't have from the beginning just to build Homefulness 'to code' and it's made it so hard for us to even build this project as poor folks," Muteado Silencio, homeless, Indigenous co-founder of Homefulness and POOR Magazine.

From the I-Hotel to Moms4Housing, moves to take back land have been met with poLice terror and guns because the ownership of Mama Earth can't be questioned in this stolen land.

Homefulness is a homeless people's solution to homelessness. It was launched in 2011 by a multi-generational, multi-racial community of homeless, migrant, disabled, and Indigenous peoples trying to create their own self-determined solution. They followed the laws set forth by the Oakland Department of Building Inspection (DBI) so it would never be a possibility for their dream to be destroyed or shut down by claims that it "wasn't up to code." This happens all the time to homeless and low-income builders. Despite their efforts, Homefulness has been plagued from the beginning by huge fees from public and private agencies like PGE and DWP as well as the city departments that oversee building and construction projects.

Last month, before the holidays, the city shut down the Homefulness building process altogether saying we "took too long" to build it. They also assessed an "impact fee" which is supposed to support low-income housing projects. And then they told Homefulness that we had to start all over again.

Thanks to intense community pressure, Homefulness just received a 30-day extension to the shut down. But in this crisis, the Homefulness project has realized that we have to speak out against these fees and the process to build. We have to try to work with conscious legislators to exempt poor and homeless people from exorbitant fees and impossible requirements which make it impossible for us to manifest our own solutions and stay in our neighborhoods and communities. To date, Homefulness has created sustainable and safe housing for four houseless families and disabled elders, a school for homeless children, a sliding scale cafe for the community to eat healthy food, and a poor and homeless people-run radio station.

"Affordable housing is not affordable. Section 8 vouchers are useless. And when poor people build our own homes, we get hit by thousand dollar permits over and over to come to the realization that the system wants to keep us chasing our tails while the city government continues to red tape our hands behind our back. Thus, turning us back to the streets as they continue to play footsie with million dollar developers who are giving a green light to build multi-million dollar luxury condos with no low-income buy in.," said Leroy Moore, formerly homeless, disabled co-founder of Homefulness and POOR Magazine.

"Six years ago, before I left DBI, they said they were trying to become more "business-like," said Bill Durham, long-time Oakland resident who was gentrified out of his neighborhood and stood with POOR Magazine to manifest this change. "After, they said that permits got more expensive. I didn't even understand what they meant. I thought we were there to serve the people of Oakland," Bill concluded.

"When the city swept our encampment they claimed our curbside homes weren't "up to code" which is how the city rationalized demolishing them," said Alfred Estrada, currently houseless after multiple sweeps and demolitions of encampments he was staying in.

We poor and homeless people will not give up or give in to the same colonial forces that made us houseless in the first place. But we cannot stay silent about this anymore and we have no more money for these exorbitant fees. So, we are beginning a series of legislative visits to change this set-up from the get-up situation for poor, working class, and homeless builders in Oakland. Please stand with us. Please join us as we continue the work of UnSElling Mama Earth and UngentriFUKing our neighborhoods and our lives.

"Maybe you shouldn't be building this project..." Is the City of Oakland Really Doing All They Can To Create Affordable Housing?

Bridget Cervelli
June 15, 2021

"You owe $72,000 for these water and sewer permits," said the East Bay Municipal Water District (EBMUD) clerk.

"We don't have that kind of money," replied organizers from POOR Magazine's Homefulness project.

"Well maybe you shouldn't be building this project then..." the EBMUD clerk replied and then, without waiting for a response, walked away.

For nearly 10 years, organizers at POOR Magazine, a poor/houseless/ Black, Brown, and Indigenous people-led grassroots organization

HHHH

deep in the heart of East Oakland, have been building Homefulness, a permanent housing solution with 8 no-cost housing units for formerly houseless individuals and families.

Oakland has publicly committed to taking our housing crisis seriously, and you can read all about plans to tackle it on the city's website. They list providing deeply affordable housing as one of their priorities. It doesn't get more affordable than free, but Homefulness has taken 10+ years to build due mostly to an endless barrage of permit and inspection fees, impossible timelines, and fines for taking too long to pay.

> "[In 2019] before the holidays, [the City of Oakland] shut down the Homefulness building process all together saying we 'took too long' to build, and assessed an 'impact fee' which is supposed to support low-income housing projects, as well as told us we had to start all over again."
>
> *Tiny aka Lisa Gray-Garcia, formerly houseless parent, author, and POOR Magazine Co-Founder*

POOR Magazine runs entirely on donations, occasional grants, and the support of POOR's Solidarity Family, people with privilege who donate time and money and have usually taken classes at POOR. Over the 20+ years POOR Magazine has been in existence they have developed prolific arts, education and child care programs such as Deecolonize Academy, F.A.M.I.L.Y (Family Access to Multi-Cultural Intergenerational Learning with our Youth) and POOR Press, where they self-publish literature that directly impacted participants produce. They also consistently provide free food, hygiene products, and other essentials to the wider community. Despite their free provision of shelter, safety, and services to Oaklanders in most need, appeals to the city are met again and again with rejection. It was only after intense community pressure that Homefulness was given a 30-day extension to raise funds and continue building in 2019.

> "The City has been charging us several thousands of dollars we don't have from the beginning just to build Homefulness, and it's made it so hard for us to even build this project as poor and homeless people. "
>
> *Muteado Silencio, houseless, indigenous Co-Founder of Homefulness and POOR Magazine*

Sustainable Economies Law Center (SELC) has been representing POOR Magazine in their ongoing struggle with the City of Oakland to build no-cost housing for our unhoused community members. Most recently, they drafted a letter requesting relaxation of a requirement for 3 unneeded parking spaces that would require $25,000 to pay for sidewalk cuts and grading. The letter cited that Homefulness is rent free, helping to meet Oakland's desperate need for affordable housing, and is located on a major transit corridor. Residents are extremely low and no-income and most do not have cars. SELC noted that the new parking spaces would eliminate 2 badly needed public parking spaces and eliminate space earmarked for a community garden.

The legal team attached a report by the American Planning Association, People Over Parking. The City's parking requirements contradict not only their public commitment to prioritize affordable housing, but a growing awareness of the undue burden that parking requirements place on construction of affordable housing. Cities nationwide have adopted the elimination of parking requirements, notably here at home in San Francisco where all parking requirements were eliminated in 2018 and in Berkeley where the City Council voted to eliminate all parking requirements for new residential construction.

The response from the City was a suggestion that we either change the zoning law or begin the process for a "variance," with an application cost alone of over $3,000. Both are hugely time consuming and highly politicized processes that unhoused community members cannot afford to wait for.

There is no guarantee of variance approval and no guarantee that other similar unexpected costs would arise as the City's private stance toward this essential housing construction consistently contradicts their public pledge to support affordable housing crucial to address the inhumanity of our housing crisis.

"The City of Oakland recently announced the beginning of a new program designed to assist low income families with a monthly grant of $500 a month for 18 months. Providing families with supplemental income for a short time will help but it is not a long-term housing solution. The City should partner with the work that Homefulness is doing by creating homes for families, a real long-term solution to the crisis that is facing thousands of people in our city. I am beseeching the City of Oakland planning department, City Officials, and the Mayor to assist Homefulness in overcoming the hurdles that are now a hindrance to the completion of the building and ultimately housing the very people that they are trying to serve with their new program."

Corrina Gould, Co-Founder and Co-Director of The Sogorea Te Land Trust, member of POOR Magazine's Elephant Council and Indian People Organizing for Change

POOR Magazine's organizers have long recognized the need for change in city housing policy and recently co-authored legislation with City

Council member At-Large, Rebecca Kaplan, that would forgive some of the prohibitive permit fees for buildings with 95% affordable housing. The legislation has received vocal support from City Council President Nikki Fortunato Bas and City Council Members Carroll Fife, Sheng Thao, and Loren Taylor, whose district includes the site of Homefulness in East Oakland. Inexplicably, the simple legislation still sits waiting for review by City Attorney Barbara Parker. In January, Kimberly Jones, Kaplan's Chief of Staff, said she was, "surprised this has taken this long. I thought by now we would have some work. They are normally quick and efficient."

> "Us poor and homeless people in the U.S. are in states of emergency—between the demolitions of thousands of units of public housing, the extreme rise in gentrification and evictions of low-income and working-class elders and families, and the concurrent rise in the criminalization of unhoused encampments and our bodies, which is why it is so urgent for people to listen to our own actual solutions to poverty and homelessness."
>
> *Tiny aka Lisa Gray-Garcia, formerly houseless single parent, author and Co-Founder of POOR Magazine*

Oakland prides itself on being a leader in social issues. The actions taken toward Homefulness belie that legacy. Our current zoning laws and fee schedule respond only to big developers but leave no room for independent builders and homeowners. It is time to make room for real Oaklanders and fast track legislation, such as that co-authored by POOR Magazine to City Council, not delay it and ignore the gaping hole in our zoning laws it responds to. We need housing for our community members who are forced to survive the trauma of the streets. This is an opportunity for the Planning Department to demonstrate leadership, listen to the needs of its community members who are providing safety, shelter, and care to our unhoused neighbors, and fulfill the City's pledge to build deeply affordable housing.

> "Affordable housing is not affordable, Section 8 vouchers are useless and when poor people build our own homes we get hit by thousands of dollars in permits over and over to come to the realization that the system wants to keep us chasing our tails while city government continues to red tape our hands behind our back thus turning us back to the streets as they continue to play footsies with million dollar developers who are given a green light to build multimillion-dollar luxury condos with no low-income buy in."
>
> *Leroy Moore, formerly houseless, disabled Co-Founder of Krip-Hop Nation, and POOR Magazine*

Testimony by Lisa "Tiny" Gray-Garcia of POOR Magazine regarding delays to the construction of Homefulness at 8032 MacArthur

September 13, 2021

Dear City of Oakland,

For nearly 10 years, organizers at POOR Magazine, a poor/houseless/Black, Brown and Indigenous people-led grassroots organization deep in the heart of East Oakland(Occupied Ohlone/Lisjan lands), have been building Homefulness, a permanent housing solution with 4 rent-free housing units (with poverty scholarship informed healing, education, advocacy and art support services on-site) for unhoused, disabled individuals, elders and families. This project has not been

undertaken for any reason other than to provide lifesaving shelter to individuals and families currently surviving life on the streets with no practical pathway to housing.

There is no question that the housing crisis in Oakland puts lives at risk. No one understands this better than the ever-increasing population of Oakland residents living outside, exposed to the elements, sweeps, violence and every other danger that comes when residents have no way to find shelter throughout the night. The builders at POOR Magazine, all of us are currently or formerly unhoused, believe that no one should have to survive this kind of risk, a sentiment the City of Oakland claims to share. This 24 year old organization, responsible for consistently providing prolific arts and education programs, vital resources and a community of support to poor and unhoused Bay Area residents, has spent the past 10 years putting every resource at our disposal toward the effort of creating life-saving shelter and services at Homefulness.

POOR Magazine has always existed and functioned in community with a vast network of unhoused organizers nation-wide as well as unhoused Oakland residents, many of whom were born here in

Oakland and pushed into the streets with the economic hardships and house-grabbing development trends that are no secret to anyone. These trends, endemic to capitalistic patterns of development, are part of the reason that POOR Magazine's builders operate with strict adherence to guidance from First Nations peoples and a Matriarchal, intergenerational "Elephant Council" that has been built over the decades to make decisions and navigate the crises that consistently arise for unhoused communities whose very existence is criminalized. Our spiritual and community-oriented practices guide the operation and organizing ethos that define POOR Magazine. These values, traditions and spiritual practices are non-negotiable as we provide a solution to the daily traumas poor and unhoused people endure as a consequence of the status quo capitalistic values that have driven us to this inexcusable housing crisis. They are also the very reason that POOR Magazine must function entirely on donations, occasional grants, and the support of POOR's Solidarity Family, people with privilege who donate time and money after taking a series of seminars at POOR's PeopleSkool where they learn about the decolonizing principles informed by an original theory we created called *Poverty Scholarship- Poor People-led Theory, Art, Words and Tears Across Mama Earth-*(creating curriculum from

the book of the same name) by which POOR Magazine operates. The inherent value of an organization modeling a human-centered rather than money-centered way of operating is recognized by the vast community of people who support POOR Magazine.

Understanding all of this is essential for City officials to comprehend as they question why Homefulness has not been able to conform to the deadlines larger, wealthy developers are accustomed to. The City's very narrow process of development leaves no room for builders who are not a part of a multimillion dollar development operation. Throughout construction, POOR has had to navigate this process with no support, financially or logistically, from the City of Oakland. In fact, Homefulness builders have encountered only obstacles from the City; financial, bureaucratic, and emotional, as we have been discouraged, time and again, by employees of the City and semi-public agencies (such as EBMUD and PG&E) who have expressed disdain when members of POOR Magazine are unfamiliar with a process or fail to have tens of thousands of dollars on hand to pay for unforeseen costs. The emotional toll is significant for people, already taxed from the unrelenting demands of survival poor and unhoused people contend with, who encounter hostility, discrimination and endless expensive and unfamiliar obstacles from a City that claims to prioritize the creation of shelter.

It is important for all of this to be taken into consideration in regards to the timeline of the Homefulness housing development. Unfortunately, the City's process allows for none of these very human realities, as is evident by their seemingly oblivious inquiry as to a singular cause of delay, date of interruption and date that construction was renewed. This is an unreasonable question, hostile in itself when considering that this has been a 10 year process during which Homefulness builders have been completely transparent and asked consistently for help and guidance to no avail. It is from this understanding that we lay out for you the **multiple, overlapping obstacles that have caused construction of Homefulness to take so much longer than the City's process of development allows for.**

The building and planning process for Homefulness began in 2010, when POOR Magazine builders began meeting with Architecture for Humanity to develop building plans. After months of meetings, we created a mock up and found that the project would cost $2.5 million. While the planning and visioning from these meetings is a relevant part of the Homefulness process, the cost of working with the Architecture for Humanity Architects was unrealistic for a poor and houseless people-led, donation based organization to count on being able to fundraise. Not to mention that we were unfamiliar with "Natural Building" a truly "green" ancient technology dream, rooted in the indigenous, ancestors-led values of us, the founders/co-builders at POOR Magazine. So a search was begun for an architect who held this knowledge as well as supported POOR's vision of an anti-capitalistic, free-housing development and could work with our limited funding. The next year, in 2011, POOR connected with our current architect, Bob Theis, an experienced natural builder, and began meeting with the zoning department, approximately seven times, to get a sense of what plans would be acceptable. Part of this process was taking those conversations with Planning back to POOR's Inter-generational Elephant Council and Revolutionary Building Circles to strategize a way to move forward in line with both City policy and the spiritual principles and community values that guide POOR's work.

After much prayer, ceremony and deliberation, POOR's Elephant Council (their Inter-Tribal, multi-generation decision-making body) decided to proceed with construction of our original vision, a straw bale housing project. This ancient type of construction has enjoyed a revival since the 1990's in North America, Europe and Australia due to an increased awareness of environmental issues. The sustainability, energy efficiency, natural fire retardant qualities and high insulation value were ideal not just for the Homefulness community, but for all of Oakland. In September of 2012, POOR entered into pre-planning discussions with the City. In December 2012 we submitted plans. In October 2014, Planning approved them. For four years, POOR was engaged in construction of straw bale houses. The whole time, we were operating in conversation with the City, who offered guidance and outright approval (linked above). During this stage of planning we spent about $40,000 to begin the process of getting inspections, asphalt lifting and checking the soil. The builders held several ceremonies on the land as was necessary for the process that honored their commitment to non-colonizing development as outlined in community with the Indigenous leaders, prayer givers, cultural workers, artists and community members vested in the project. Plans were made with ongoing collaboration specifically from Oakland Indigenous community leaders like Corrina Gould, an Ohlone leader and co-founder of the First People's, women-owned Sogorea Te' Land Trust. Corrina joined POOR's collective decision-making body, the Elephant Council, to join the two organizations' (Sogorea Te' Land Trust and POOR Magazine) efforts to develop innovative processes of envisioning land use that counters capitalistic patterns of development that perpetuate the colonization, racism and classism that have left Indigenous, poor, black, disabled and other marginalized populations unhoused.

On December 27, 2013, Homefulness builders submitted plans to the Planning Department/Building Dept. When the plans were submitted to Building and Permits, they rejected the submittal, stating

the plans presented a fire hazard. Homefulness builders were told that for the plans to be approved, we would need to get a $10,000 fire safe test, and that even with the test, it was unlikely the straw-bale plans would pass. **This was the first of several instances in which POOR Magazine was blindsided by an obstacle from the City that we expected would have been raised in pre-planning conversations with the Planning Department.** As new builders with lived experience of housing instability, POOR Magazine's crew wanted to be sure that everything was done in accordance with City policy. The expectation from having the pre-planning conversation with the City was that all costs, permits and potential obstacles would be raised in that conversation so that upon submission, the builders would be prepared to move forward expeditiously.

The unexpected hurdle of the costly fire safe test is also an example of an expectation that POOR should spend thousands of dollars on applications for inspection or exception to unreasonable costly requirements without any guarantee of approval (such as the later suggestion to apply for a variance to the City's requirement that we build parking spaces that car-less residents would not use). POOR Magazine has no "budget" but rather raises money for what I have dubbed UnSelling Mama Earth and therefore absolutely does not have thousands of dollars we can afford to spend on uncertain applications or processes. Even without the cost of application, these kinds of upsets still required a costly pivot to plans that would eliminate the need for the unexpected application expense. **Because of the City's unexpected rejection of POOR Magazine's straw-bale plans, we had to scrap the plans entirely, which carried a significant loss of time and effort, much of which was donated by professionals and community members doing work for free to support the Homefulness project. This detracted substantially from the resources later available to support our building efforts under the 2016 building permit at issue in our Application for Waiver of Impact Fees.**

POOR Magazine does not have tens of thousands of dollars in excess lying around to cover unforeseen costs we reasonably expected to be warned about in pre-planning conversations. While the City has emphasized that a lack of funds is not an acceptable reason for delay, when costs are encountered without warning, the City's requirement that builders be able to pay without delay becomes unreasonable. POOR Magazine has been consistent in proceeding with transparency and requests for guidance from City Departments specifically so that we could be sure to move forward in compliance and be prepared for unexpected costs. Unfortunately, the City never provided support navigating the building process in this way and most unexpected costs were imposed without warning.

After a new process of coming up with plans in community and in accordance with the spiritual practices that guide all land-use activities that POOR Magazine engages in, new plans were drawn up. In 2015, Homefulness submitted new plans for approval of the four-unit construction. A year later, on May 2, 2016 these plans were approved, but a new Impact Fee went into effect months later, which made Homefulness potentially liable for tens of thousands of dollars in impact fees if we did not complete the project within three years. The most expensive impact fee, the Affordable Housing one, is supposed to serve the purpose of supporting construction of affordable housing. As Homefulness is 100% free housing, POOR Magazine reasonably expected that these fees would be excused. Especially when considering that Homefulness is the kind of development that should have benefitted from the Impact Fees imposed on for-profit developers.

Notoriously, the City has failed to impose Impact Fees appropriately on large developers. POOR Magazine builders were also never made aware that these fees were designed to support construction projects like Homefulness, symptomatic of the ineffectiveness of the Impact Fee policy that has been commented on publicly by City Officials like Rebecca Kaplan and leadership in community organizations such as East Bay Housing Organization's Policy Director Jeff Levin, among others. This San Francisco Chronicle article from 2019 documents our publicly stated concerns, as well as the concerns of City Council President, Nikki Fortunato Bas and others: "Oakland created an affordable housing fee 3 years ago. Developers haven't built a single unit yet." Here is a 2019 article from the *East Bay Times*, that raises similar concerns about the lack of sensible imposition of Impact Fees and failure to use fees collected to support affordable housing development: "Oakland failing to collect significant amount of affordable housing fees it's entitled to: Affordable housing and market-rate developers question how much the city is saying it is collecting from affordable housing impact fees." Reference is made to an audit of the Impact Fee process that should have had a publicly available draft ready in 2020. Homefulness builders were unable to find a copy of the audit draft, but suspect that our development project may serve as a case-study demonstrating the failure of Oakland's Impact Fee policy to serve its intended purpose.

Another significant financial hurdle that was unreasonable for the City to expect Homefulness to cover with no warning came in 2017. Prior to 2017, all plans had been made to complete construction unit by unit. In 2017, POOR Magazine learned that this plan would not be accepted and we would have to construct all four townhomes at once. Our urgent fundraising from POOR Magazine's poverty skolaz was almost impossible and caused us once again to slow down. Eventually with support from our "Solidarity Family" graduates and alumni of PeopleSkool, who co-organize other people with privilege, we were finally able to raise $300,000 to accommodate this shift. This

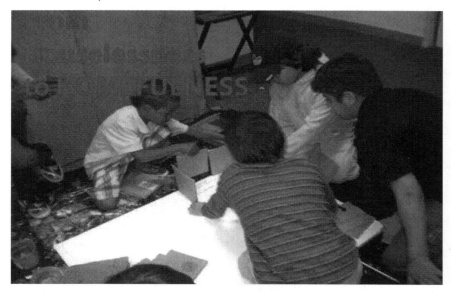

demonstrates the level of community support for construction of Homefulness and the process by which we proceed.

In addition to endless exorbitant fees and obstacles from the City, **we were constantly facing problems from PG&E, EBMUD, the County Assessor, and other agencies.** In December 2016 Bridges Construction Service, Inc. (BCSI) performed an excavation to install new gas service for the new units and remove service for an existing duplex, per PG&E plans and specifications. During excavation, a PG&E inspector marked the area, but BCSI could not find any of the existing gas lines. They called PG&E to come and re-mark the area again. After a few test holes, PG&E found the existing gas line under the second PG&E locator's markings, and confirmed that the first markings had been in error. In February 2018, POOR filed a claim, with help from BCSI and at the suggestion of the PG&E inspector who discovered his predecessor's error. In all, including the cost of safety and traffic control to work around gas lines that didn't exist, **PG&E's error cost the Homefulness builders $16,000 and significant time and stress.**

In 2016, we encountered another hurdle. The Alameda County Assessor took away our property tax exemption for 8032 MacArthur, despite POOR Magazine having had this exemption for the previous three years, with no disqualifying change in POOR Magazine's project programming. This situation pulled Homefulness' attention away from construction work in order to find a pro bono law firm to address the issue. We hired the DLA Piper law firm in June 2016, and put energy toward recovering this exemption, a situation that remains unresolved.

Another hurdle arose in May 2018, when EBMUD incorrectly demanded $72,000 for water service, a higher cost than the $60,000 initially quoted to POOR Magazine. The additional $12,000 was due to imposition of higher rates that newer developments are charged. POOR Magazine was initially told this cost was increased because we were being penalized for not paying $60,000 before the date of EBMUD's pricing change. **This was an error on the part of EBMUD which was later corrected, but this is an example of the kind of financial hurdles and time costs that POOR Magazine was expected**

to navigate. In this instance, several months of communication ensued before the mistake was corrected.

The community of currently and formerly houseless, indigenous builders involved in the Homefulness project would have benefited immensely from simple guidance from City officials. This guidance is something that has finally been promised at this late stage of development now that POOR Magazine has enlisted the support of community members experienced in working in Building and Planning for the City of Oakland, and after sustained pressure and inquiries to City Officials from POOR Magazine supporters. For the past ten years, Homefulness builders have had to navigate development processes alone and encountered disdain and discouragement from unsympathetic representatives of the City and agencies associated with the building process (such as EBMUD and PG&E). Where we expected to find encouragement for construction of badly needed rent-free housing, we were met with consistent refusals by the City to help understand the building process or dismiss unreasonable and costly requirements (like the imposition of Impact Fees and costly parking construction that would not be used by residents without cars).

Community builders, such as the team from POOR Magazine, do not have the years of experience and deep pockets of large developers the City is accustomed to dealing with. At many points in the Homefulness building process, there are examples of how the City's policies exclude anyone other than large developers or wealthy individuals from reasonably complying with their timelines, costs and lack of guidance. POOR Magazine representatives have had extensive conversations with City Officials who acknowledge that the obstacles Homefulness builders have faced are unreasonable. Current building, planning and zoning policies are widely recognized as ineffective at supporting construction of affordable housing, and could be improved based on lessons learned with Homefulness.

Rather than sticking to processes and fees that City Officials have admitted are unreasonable and threaten to derail completion of Homefulness, free housing that stands empty and built to code, the City could choose to prioritize the safety of constituents by allowing them to move into Homefulness. It is hard to understand the City's commitment to obtuse policies that prolong the danger that unsheltered families face while they wait for the OK to move into Homefulness.

Homefulness has always been created as a poor, indigenous and houseless people-led solution and vision to offer as a model for change all across Turtle Island (US). Everything we are struggling with will be taught and shared with cities and states struggling with the violence of sweeps, poor people-hate and homelessness. Currently there are three other cities following and re-creating our model: Bellingham, WA, Bend, OR, and Corpus Christie, TX. These delays are absolute violence in this time of so much struggle. We urge the City to act differently, to show themselves to be models of change, not models of more violence, and to prioritize the safety of constituents and the construction of affordable housing by approving Homefulness and beginning the process of changing policies that are effectively blocking poor and houseless people from occupying safe, no-cost housing.

The Homefulness Permits Process

Transcription from a Conversation with Tiny Gray-Garcia

The process of getting Homefulness approved by the city shows how Mama Earth is sold and pimped and played by an incestuous relationship between the government, private corporapetions, and papered architects, engineers, and "contractors." It's more than just the city. This is an entire building industry that's built about us without us—intentionally as fuck.

First thing, we couldn't even start building without architectural plans by a papered architect, not an indigenous architect. We had to find an architectural firm and deal with all the weird fetishizing that comes from working with people who have the race and class privilege to get those degrees. They told us "we have the answer for you" and made a big plan that would ultimately cost $4.7 million dollars to build. After that nightmare, we found someone who was willing to do it pro-bono.

Then we needed an engineer who was papered. The discounted rate for them to sign off was $25,000. That's the kind of payment the college hustle gets you.

We had to go through extreme hoops to even get the city to look at our zoning plans and then had to shell out endless amounts of cash. It started with $29,000 in zoning permit fees. Then it was one thing after another. The city had to approve every single step we took, and always with a fee. Half the time, they said we didn't get approved, which is fine. Some stuff we really did need to get approved on.

From there, it was a huge process once our plans were approved. We needed licensed, papered building contractors because when those builders use certain machinery, they refuse to let others deal with it. The city also wouldn't approve our plans unless we used a certain quality of materials, so we had to pay tens of thousands of dollars for building supplies.

We weren't trying to be bougie. All along, we were doing revolutionary building circles where papered architects and builders were sitting with unpapered, poor people builders. We planned to build a natural building; we had a straw house vision. We wanted an actual green project in a so-called green city, but they canceled it. They

said they couldn't approve this ancient technology that never burned because it was a "fire hazard." So another huge plan ended up being totally useless and we had to redo almost 30K worth of engineering.

And then there were the inspections. We also paid tens of thousands of dollars for those—$48,000 for fire sprinklers and $30,000 more for an inspection. Some of the inspections are real. We're not saying they shouldn't do inspections. We're asking why they are charging us $8,000 for someone to come out and tell us we can install a toilet??

On top of that, we had to deal with the corporapetions that control utilities. The city's water company, East Bay Municipal Utilities District, has its own board of directors and makes massive amounts of money. They told us it would be $72,000 to put in water meters just to figure out what we would owe them. It took us almost three years to come up with the money for that. The city's electric company, Pacific Gas & Electric, charged us $62,000 just to install a box and have people come out to inspect it. We explored solar power, but they told us it would cost $80,000 to set up, and even then we'd have to link it up to a corporapetion.

The final thing that has stopped us is the $40,000 impact fee, which is a fine the city puts on big developers for taking too long to build. Like other fines the city has used to hold us hostage, the money they get from this fee is supposed to go towards "affordable housing." So the city charged us and shut us down because all the time it took us to deal with all shit they made us go through. The only reason we got a delay in having to pay was because of a backdoor connection to the mayor's office. But it's still being held over our heads.

Youth Skolaz Report: Permit Gangstas

Below are the reports from the DeeColonize Academy youth skolaz on POOR Magazine's meetings at City Hall trying to challenge the impact fees being imposed on Homefulness. Here is a petition on our behalf.

Permit Wars

In December 2019, the building process of Homefulness #1 was halted after the Permit Gangstas (City Officials) said that we had taken too long and our permit had expired. When we went to find how to fix this they said that we needed to pay $27,000 in Impact Fees. Now if you don't know what an Impact fee is, I'll tell you. An Impact Fee is a fee that people pay so that the money goes to affordable housing. WE ARE BUILDING AFFORDABLE HOUSING! We also have to start from the beginning and start on zoning.

We have always paid their fees without problems, but now we could not just let this pass by. After community pressure and WeSearch we were able to get a 30-day extension and with that extension we are trying to finish everything we can in the construction while continuing our WeSearch. In this search, we met up with Lia Azul Salaverry who is the Policy Analyst and Community Liaison of Nikki Fortunato Bas. We explained our situation to her and one of the biggest issues is that it took 8 months for the fire sprinkles and the irony of the Impact Fees.

In this conversation, Lia Salaverry said something that surprised me. She said, "We are also wondering, what is happening with Impact Fees?" Meaning, the City Council employees do not know where the Impact Fees money goes. This could end up being a bigger issue. In this conference, Leo Stegman, who was also there, was trying to explain to Lia Salaverry that, "This is not a career, it's a lifestyle." He was telling her that we aren't Berkshire Hathaway building buildings for profit, we are Homefulness building houses for people. We are doing this because of stuff we have experienced, not because we want to start a business. It's because we want to help ourselves and others.

Lia Salaverry suggested that we meet up with Bobby Lopez who already knows about us and that she would be there for us in other meetings. Tiny gave an example of what most people think of us, "Ew, you're the poor people. You must be hiding something." So, Lia will help those judgments leave by supporting us.

These last few weeks have been fast-paced and busy. We have all been trying to finish the houses. After everything we've done, including a mini protest in front of City Hall, the city still demands us to pay the Impact Fees. Keep in mind that the Impact Fees are only a small part of the payments. We still have to pay for inspections, construction supplies, and the permits themselves. This experience was one of the many that show how disorganized the system is. And this is why Poor Magazine exists. To fight it.

Akil Carrillo

Conference Meeting/Complaint (Protest)

It feels like a normal day. But first, detective Ziair Hughes and his classmates go on an adventure. We go to city hall to get justice for our project.

Back Story: December 2019. The Homefulness building process that started in 2018 has stopped. These townhomes are for "low income, no income, low wage, no wage" homeless people and people that need support. We successfully started but it is not going well mid-way. The

city official members said that we (POOR Magazine) were taking too long and our permit had expired. They said that we had to pay $27,000 for Impact Fees but that doesn't make sense because we are making affordable housing for poor people that need affordable housing. So, we went to the city council to protest and fix the problem that had occurred. At the protest, we prayed, did the four directions, and spoke about our problems. All of the youth skolaz and adult poverty skolaz spoke and we got our point across to the community.

Quotes from the conference meeting with Lia Salaverry, District 2 (policy analyst & community liaison):

"This is not a career, this is a lifestyle." —Leo Stegman

"Ew, you're the poor people. You must be hiding something." —Tiny

"I'm really here to listen to what you have to say about homelessness." —Lia Salaverry

"This is a family-run project, we don't roll with the CEO's." —Uncle Mueteado (co-builder)

"Built by the people and it's for the people." —Leroy Moore

"Doesn't understand the model to unsell mama earth." —Tiny

"And how we get this project moving forward." —Lia Salaverry

"They have lived separately but live together as a community." —Charles

"Black people and brown people that have land but it was foreclosed." —Tiny

From the protest:

"I'm Ziair. Because of these fees and the process to build and try to work with conscious legislators to exempt poor and homeless people from these huge fees and impossible requirements which make it impossible for homeless and poor people to manifest our own solutions and stay in our neighborhood communities and will be kicked out by gentrification." —Ziair

In Conclusion: Thanks to the community and poor members/POOR, Homefulness was able to get a thirty-day extension to continue building. In this crisis, the Homefulness project realized we have to speak out and keep fighting because they want us to pay other fees and they do not care if we are trying to do good by the community. When we pay their fees and when we don't have the money, then we pay the fees as poor people because they are the government, and they don't give any empathy. They just want "bloodstained dollars." And to say we have to pay permits for our own people doesn't make sense. If they stop applying this unjust pressure, we will be able to get this house done. If we were gentrifiers we would be looked at differently. But since we are poor people, they treat us different.

Ziair Hughes

Meeting With Lia Azul

"The concept is that those fees are pulled then allocated to fund public housing." Those were the words of Lia Salaverry, the community liaison and policy analyst under Councilwoman Nikki Fortunato Bas. She was talking about the Impact Fees we were there to discuss that afternoon. She looked as confused as us when we told her the fee that, like she said, was used to fund public housing (i.e., below market rate or affordable housing) was charged to us, a poor and homeless people-led building project meant to house other poor and homeless families for way below market rate. After many long years being charged exorbitant fees for every single small thing that has the name "permit" in it in the process of building Homefulness, a $27,000 Impact Fee meant to help poor people who need to be housed, was the final straw for us in Homefulness. Right now, we barely have enough money to afford the utility bills for our current residents.

Phase 2 of the Homefulness Project, the 4 townhouses that will be converted into 8 units that will house homeless and low-income families, was started in 2016. Us being poor builders with very little experience in the contracting game, had no idea how much it would cost to be allowed to start building things. Yes, we knew about permits, and yes we were aware they were going to be a lot of money. However, as we ventured further and further into this project and faced more roadblocks and obstacles, we realized how profitable the business of permit licensing really was. Every step along the way was a bill, and finally, after 4 years, we are putting a stop to this.

"Homefulness makes sense because it's built by the people for the people," said Leo Stegman in the meeting with Lia. On Tuesday, February 4th, 2020, the students of Deecolonize Academy along with the residents of Homefulness and most of the Homefulness building crew, (which conveniently happens to be Homefulness residents) launched a movement by press conference in order to prevent poor and low-income builders from being stopped completely by the giant wall which is the Impact Fee. A fee was designed to help them in the first place. We spoke about how the fee is impacting us, as a grassroots and government grantless movement and we demanded change within this system that is designed to push aside us poor people with every move. We then asked for support from whoever was watching and listening, because all of us are people from the streets housing people on the streets and the city is shutting us down.

Lia Salaverry agreed to support in any way possible and also was planning to report back to Councilwoman Bass. In my eyes, she looked like she understood the struggle we were going through and did want to help in any way. But how much she is going to help is yet to be decided. Before this, there have been a lot of people with access who claimed they were down and were going to help us yet never returned our calls after the first meeting. I'm only hoping that when Lia reports back to the Councilwoman, the Councilwoman will see the evidence presented in front of her that this is unjust, and this money-making scheme has to stop, at least for the people who the supposed fee was designed to help. By doing this action we are trying to put in effect a change in the Impact Fee, saying that it will no longer be charged to the people it is supposed to help. Also, there are gray areas in the legislation and there are no accidents in government, so those gray areas must mean something, The gray areas must be cleared and the money from the Impact Fees from big companies must be given to fund affordable housing, like Homefulness's, that is yet to be built.

"We need your office to come to our neighborhood and see what we are doing," Leroy cut in. His sentiment was reflected in everyone's faces. We left the meeting hoping that we would see some changes, but we were immediately disappointed. As soon as some of the Homefulness building crew went to the permit office, they were slapped in the face with a matter-of-fact statement claiming Homefulness still owes the $27,000 Impact Fee. After all of our fighting, it is too soon to tell whether or not Councilwoman Bass will be on our side and back us up to get the Impact Fee boot off of our neck. In addition to the Impact Fee, we also have continuous smaller fees like a $529 bill allowing us to put water meters in. This does not cover the expenses for the water meters, just allows us to put them there. So, this fight is still going. We always say here that Homefulness isn't a utopic dream or something we wish to do one day, it is something we are currently doing and struggling with.

Tiburcio Garcia

The Affordable Housing Permit Fee Waiver Legislation

OAKLAND CITY COUNCIL

ORDINANCE NO. _____ C.M.S.

INTRODUCED BY COUNCIL PRESIDENT KAPLAN

ORDINANCE AMENDING THE OAKLAND MUNICIPAL CODE CHAPTER 15.04.1.165 BY ADDING THE IMPLEMENTATION OF PERMIT FEE WAIVER PROGRAM FOR AFFORDABLE HOUSING UP TO ONE MILLION ($1,000,000) APPROPRIATED FROM FUND 2415 AND WITH DISBURSEMENTS OF A MAXIMUM OF $45,000 PER PROJECT UNDER 25 UNITS AND A MAXIMUM OF $65,000 PER PROJECT OVER 26 UNITS

WHEREAS, Oakland is suffering from a serious housing crisis as housing costs in the City increase drastically, making housing at all levels of affordability and particularly affordable housing scarce and unavailable for many Oakland residents; and

WHEREAS, according to the 2019 EveryOne Counts! Homeless Point-in-Time Count homelessness grew 47% in the City of Oakland from 2017-2019, with now 4,071 individuals living in shelters or unhoused; and

WHEREAS, in Resolution 87610 C.M.S., the Oakland City Council declared a local emergency exists due to the welfare and safety concerns of those who live in homelessness or at risk of homelessness; and

WHEREAS, according to the 2019 "Oakland At Home Update; A Progress Report on Implementing the Oakland Housing Cabinet's "17K/17K" Recommendations," the City Housing Cabinet had set the expectation of new affordable housing construction to be 28% however only 8% of current new construction is affordable with the remaining 92% market-rate; and

WHEREAS, in 2019, when the Redwood Hill Townhomes affordable development project offered their 28 units to the public, there were 4,000 applicants, thereby showing the overwhelming need for new affordable housing construction; and

WHEREAS, the global COVID-19 Pandemic is exacerbating our homelessnescrisis as individuals need appropriate shelter to "shelter in place;" and

WHEREAS, in California over a 1 million people have applied for unemployment benefits because of COVID-19, thereby putting into question the ability of Oakland residents to afford an already unaffordable housing market and increasing the number of individuals at risk of homelessness;

WHEREAS, in 2001, with Ordinance 12344.C.M.S., the Oakland City Council passed the "Building Permit Fee Waiver Program" as one of several incentives to encourage seismic retrofit work for residential buildings in response to the potential devastation foreseen by earthquakes; and

WHEREAS, in 2019, Resolution 87759 C.M.S. authorized the Biennial Budget for Fiscal Years 2019-2021 and appropriating certain funds to provide for the expenditures proposed, including "waive permit inspection fees for solar power, grey water, and, affordable housing (including ADU) that commit to rent Section 8;" and

WHEREAS, the creation of an "Affordable Housing Building Permit Fee Waiver Program" is one of several incentives to encourage the completion and construction of affordable housing projects to provide habitable and appropriate living situations for those who are unhoused, in shelters, or at risk of homelessness; and

NOW, THEREFORE, THE COUNCIL OF THE CITY OF OAKLAND DOES ORDAIN AS FOLLOWS:

SECTION 1. **Recitals.** The City Council of the City of Oakland hereby determines that the preceding recitals are true and correct and an integral part of the Council's decision, and   hereby adopts and incorporates them into this Ordinance.

SECTION 2. **Purpose and Intent.** It is the purpose and intent of this Ordinance to expressly enact a temporary building permit waiver program to accelerate affordable housing construction.

SECTION 3. **Enactment of Amendments to the Oakland Municipal Code.** The Amendments are hereby enacted, to the Oakland Municipal Code Chapter 15.04.1.165, and set forth below. Chapter and section numbers and titles are indicated in bold type. Additions are indicated by underline and deletions are shown as strikethrough. Provisions of Chapter 15.04.1.165 not included herein or not shown in underline or strikethrough type are unchanged.

15.04.1.165—Fees.

A. General. Permit, plan review, processing, investigation, abatement and other relevant fees shall be established and assessed in accordance with the Master Fee Schedule and paid to the City of Oakland at time of submittal of the permit application for review or at other times as provided herein. Unpaid fees for work performed may be recovered in the manner prescribed in section 15.04.1.130.B of this Code.

B. Additional. Whenever plans, calculations, computations, reports, or other required data are incomplete or changed so as to require additional review and/or processing; or whenever valuation of work has changed or has been re-evaluated based upon inspection, additional fees as established in accordance with the Master Fee Schedule shall be assessed.

C. Refunds.

1. The Building Official may authorize the refunding of fees erroneously assessed and paid.

2. The Building Official may authorize the refunding of not more than eighty percent (80%) of fees validly assessed and paid when no work by the City has been done either under a permit application or an issued permit. Fees designated as non-refundable shall not be refunded. Fees validly assessed and paid shall not be refunded more than one-hundred eighty (180) days after expiration of a permit application or an issued permit.

3. All requests for refunds shall be submitted on a City of Oakland form and shall be accompanied by the original receipt of payment.

D. An "Affordable Housing Building Permit Fee Waiver Program" shall be implemented to waive all building permit fees for any residential building permit application with more than 95% of its units designated for low income and very low income as defined by HUD and as memorialized in a deed or other similar agreement. This extends to land trusts and landless movements where the tenants receive housing in exchange for work collectively for the benefit of the property. Up to one million ($1,000,000) from Fund 2415 shall be used to cover the fees until such time that no funds exist. Funds shall be dispersed as follows: a maximum of $45,000 per project at 25 units or under; and a maximum of $65,000 per project over 25 units. The building permit fees waived shall be based on those fees in the latest adopted City of Oakland Master Fee Schedule related to Planning and Building Department fees including, without limitation, Administration Items A through E- Permit Application Fee; Plan Check Fees; and Inspection Fees. This shall sunset by January 1, 2022.

SECTION 4. **Severability.** If any article, part, section, subsection, sentence, clause, or phrase of this Ordinance be held to be invalid or unconstitutional, the offending portion shall be severed and shall not affect the validity of remaining portions which shall remain in full force and effect. The City Council of the City of Oakland hereby declares that it would have approved and adopted this ordinance and each article, part, section, subsection, sentence, clause, and phrase thereof irrespective of the fact that any one or more articles, parts, sections, subsections, sentences, clauses, phrases or other parts be declared unconstitutional.

SECTION 5. **Effective Date.** This Ordinance shall be effective immediately on final adoption if it receives six or more affirmative votes; otherwise it shall become effective upon the seventh day after final adoption by the City Council.

SECTION 6. **Conforming Changes.** The City Council hereby authorizes the City Administrator or designee to make non-substantive, technical conforming changes (essentially correction of typographical and clerical errors), prior to formal publication of the Amendments in the Oakland Municipal Code.

IN COUNCIL, OAKLAND, CALIFORNIA,
PASSED BY THE FOLLOWING VOTE:
AYES — FORTUNATO BAS, GALLO, GIBSON MCELHANEY, KALB,
     REID, TAYLOR, THAO AND PRESIDENT KAPLAN
NOES —
ABSENT —
ABSTENTION —
ATTEST: LATONDA SIMMONS
     City Clerk and Clerk of the Council of the City of Oakland,
     California

Building Homefulness

Breaking Ground

Construction

Photos by Muteado Silencio

Land Trust (IN WHAT??) Transforming Land Trusts into LiberationOfLand (Trusts)

Tiny Gray-Garcia
September 16, 2019

Land trust ?
Trust in What?
U see my broken unhoused mind is CONfused by
Grant deeds, mortgages, Probate and leases
All meant to steal
Mama Earth from mama earth's peoples—

(excerpt from Liberation Not Trust)

"In the US, all the laws around property rights actually are there to serve and support the business interests of developers, speculators and realtors, even land trusts aren't safe." The young lawyer who was teaching us houseless/formerly houseless poverty skolaz at POOR Magazine the twisted lies known as real estate law ended his speech and shook his head. We had called him in to help us set up the legal structure of our plan to spiritually and legally un-sell the small parcel of Mama Earth we were building called Homefulness, but now we all felt more depressed than we were before he started.

In this occupied land, one of the hardest "lessons" this poverty skola has had to "learn," as a houseless child and then later as a single parent struggling with eviction, then homelessness, poverty, and constant and ongoing gentriFUKation in San Francisco, Oakland and LA, is that every single part of the settler colonizer lies (laws) that govern stolen Turtle Island, protect, support, lift-up, enable, and promote the buying, selling, and profiting off of Mama Earth.

Beginning with the original "lie of discovery" which is analogous to someone stealing the jacket off your back and turning around and proclaiming they "found a jacket" and making a whole series of fake stories about how they found it, and laws to keep stealing all of your jackets and every other article of clothing you own and while they are at it—you. The road to Mama Earth theft and the paper and politricks in place to cover it up is long and intentionally complicated.

From LLC's to CONservatorShit, guardianship, mortgages, loans, probate kkkort (court) to wills, there is an endless series of codes, regulations, and laws meant to CONfuse, jam up, disorient, and cover up the ongoing theft of Mama Earth from Black, Brown, Indigenous, and poor people.

Folks work their entire lives (often in boring/ back-breaking, hard jobs they don't like) to achieve a success model based on the acquisition and then hoarding of Mama Earth. Her resources and stacks of paper with dead wite men on them, being constantly told that once they do, as in the case of the Sloan family of North Oakland and the Vasquez family of Fresno, just to name two of literally millions of working class people in this country, the kkkorts and laws steal it away in a bloody river of paper.

Add to this the violent reality of the demolition and eradication of all of the public housing projects through more politricks from the benignly named RAD program, insane gentrifUKation everywhere, the subsequent rise in people having to live unhoused, and then the criminalization of so-called public spaces so unhoused people can't even sit or stand while houseless anywhere. The fix is in and continues to get worse. Lately, we have SB35 by Scott Weiner enabling the insane high rise condos and rich people rental projects as long as they include an eensy-teensy bit of "affordable" housing which actually isn't affordable for ANYONE low-income.

This all brings us to the lie of Land Trusts. Which isn't really a lie even though the two "L's" sound good together. It's really what people, organizations, and gentriFUKation victims are told—it is all we have to combat the ongoing War On the Poor. What we aren't told is that all of these lies (laws) and codes, even land trusts are embedded in a predatory system meant to power the wealth-hoarders and land-stealers, speculators, and bankkksters.

Danza Azteca prayer from Coatlique Calpulli in the all nations Mama Earth prayer at the Bank of Come-Unity Reparations Ceremonial Launch

In the case of a whole gaggle of violent evictions faced by elders and families in gentriFUKation city (SF) and Oakland lately, local land trusts have swooped in with love and respect trying in earnest to save peoples' homes so more stories of eviction as elder abuse and ultimately death like Iris Canada and Ron Likkers doesn't happen. Land trusts theoretically take the land off the real snake market so the tenants don't end up on the street, which is true. But what people don't know is that like all the other colonizer-created lies (laws) they have an expiration date. Sometimes they are short, 15, 25, or 50 years. Sometimes they are much longer, for 99 years. They are also rife with all the same loopholes that enable wealth-hoarders to hide and protect resources. They also enable the eventual sale, transfer, and/or return back to the real snake market when the board transitions, the trust runs out, or the entity holding it in the trust sells its interest in the land.

What people rarely understand or overstand is that the roots of all the devil-oper trees are rotten. The laws on the books are ALL meant to confuse and steal and hide for profit Mama Earth. What actually needs to happen is to purely stop that violence in its tracks, to un-sell and/or rematriate, as the wise land liberators of the Ohlone/Lisjan Nation of Oakland call their work, to spiritually and legally un-sell Mama Earth as we are doing at Homefulness, and hold in what we are calling a LiberationofLand Trust.

This is not an easy thing to do and requires one to work closely with a conscious lawyer and, equally important, work closely with ancestors, poverty skolaz, and First Nations peoples of the land and set up a stewardship, rather than perpetuate the violence of an owner-ship. The badass folks at East Bay Permanent Real Estate Cooperative are also trying this notion out. And as of now, they are still working within the land trust model but at least are clearly offensively liberating tracks of land out of krapitalist ownership.

The Sogorea Te Land Trust, led by native women has clearly stated in their purpose statement, a completely different way to conceptualize use of Mama Earth.

Sogorea Te is an urban Indigenous women-led land trust based in the SF Bay Area that returns Indigenous land to Indigenous people. Through the practices of rematriation, cultural revitalization, and land restoration, STLT calls on native and non-native peoples to heal and transform legacies of colonization, genocide, and patriarchy and to do the work our ancestors and future generations are calling us to do.

For us landless/houseless, incarcerated, bordered, criminalized, disabled, evicted, and gentrifUKed, multi-nationed, multi-cultural Black, Brown, and pan-Indigenous poverty skolaz at POOR Magazine, the **LiberationOfLandTrust** is what we are slowly manifesting, building, and realizing. Which isn't to say it is just houses for house-less families and elders (which it is) but it is also a consciousness shift away from the harmful, extractive system that is Krapitalism (capitalism). The LiberationofLandTrust is rooted in all the things we are intentionally un-taught in krapitalism's cult of individualism, scarcity models and separation nation, which isn't good for anyone but is especially bad for poor people and worse for houseless people and even worse for Mama Earth herself.

In the LiberationofLandTrust, we take Mama Earth off of the realEsnake market for good in a combination of legal, cultural, and spiritual work to protect Mama Earth and her earth peoples, with the knowledge that if we stopped buying and selling Mama Earth we wouldn't have homelessness or fires in the Amazon or extraction in the Jamaica or sacred site desecration or gentriFUKation or removal or....

The LiberationofLandTrust is launched first with permission, prayer, and leadership/inclusion from First Nations peoples of wherever that part of Mama Earth is. A long prayerful process culminating in a Peoples Agreement is created among the peoples that launch it, and multi-nationed prayer ceremonies from the people's traditions of the neighborhood and the residents of that neighborhood, and is ultimately rooted in the poor people theory we call Poverty Scholarship as well as love, Mama Earth protection, and humility. Most importantly, all the people involved have to commit to the value of life not profit and all residents agree to never submit/convert to the lie of "rent." Meaning, a contribution to the costs of un-selling and stewarding Mama Earth will be shared but rent will never be charged and equally importantly the violence of "speculation" and development will never be perpetrated and the state (aka poLice/politricksters) will never be called in to "solve" our problems for us.

After all the spiritual and cultural labor, which is intense, then an entity or group must also focus on a matrix of legal manifestations to protect their small parcel of Mama Earth from the lies put in place to steal, destroy, hoard, extract, and profit off of her. These are not easy and will take the work of a papered and a jailhouse/community advocate like so many of us Po folks have to become to survive, all to ensure that as many bases are covered as possible to prevent future speculation. (A template POOR Magazine poverty skolaz share with other poor and Indigenous groups as a workshop.)

And lastly but definitely not leastly, this includes the tireless hard solidarity work of conscious folks with race/class/formal education privilege working together, sharing resources, blood-stained dollars, and something we at POOR Magazine call "Community Reparations." We teach on Community Reparation in the Poverty Scholarship textbook and at PeopleSkool, which we share with anyone who is interested in the concept of Radical Redistribution and helped to launch the herstory-making Bank of Come-Unity Reparations.

These might seem like utopic ideas or some cutesy hippie notion but they are actually rooted in the shared extreme terror of the state, of the eviction Nation, and the impact of removal, homelessness, criminalization, speculation, and land/resource theft of poor, Black, Brown, Indigenous, and working class people that happens everyday in amerikkka.

While Mama Earth's forests are intentionally burned and un-contacted, Indigenous peoples are uprooted and evicted from their ancestral lands from India to the Amazon, from East Oakland to Kashmir. Please listen when I shout that we are all in "statesofEmergency" so there is truly no more time to keep doing things the same old same old. It is time to lead with decolonial, degentriFUKing values, so we can collectively hold onto, lift up, and liberate the small parts of Mama Earth that are still here, for her ancestors and all of us.

Land trust ?
Trust in What?
U see my broken unhoused mind is CONfused by
Grant deeds, mortgages, , Probate and leases
All meant to steal
Mama Earth from mama earths peoples—

(excerpt from Liberation Not Trust)

knives made of paper called treaties and LLCCCC's

Created by colonizer stealers

Bloody history
Led by wite Jesus toting missionaries
Endless theft of mama earth
gilded with false deities

Claiming discovery of something already inhabited, cared for
centuries by Original bodies

527 years later we have indigenous children and elders kept in
    cages
Eviction of 100 year old African sages and the violence of
    bulldozers
destroying our homes, stealing our belongings and
    incarcerating our babies

An Innovative, Truly Green Vision of Housing and Land Use in Oakland for Homeless Families and Youth created by Homeless Families and Youth in Oakland

Press Release

Low-income and homeless Indigenous youth, families and elders in collaboration with preeminent natural building experts, architects and engineers present an innovative housing and land-use project for themselves and other very low-income, displaced and homeless families

> **What:** Press Conference
> **When:** TODAY—12:30 p.m. Monday, December 21, 2015
> **Where:** Oscar Grant Plaza in front of Oakland
> City Hall, 14th & Broadway, Oakland, CA

"Homefulness is a visionary model of how to create affordable, sustainable housing and community at a time when we, in Oakland, could not need it more. Not only that, this effort is being led by formerly homeless and under-housed people setting a powerful example for all of us," said Dunya Alwan, one of the innovative artists/architectural designers working on the Homefulness project.

131

After an 18-year journey of struggle, poverty, homelessness and displacement, the poor, Indigenous and disabled people who lead the nonprofit, grassroots arts organization POOR Magazine launched Homefulness—a truly green, amazingly innovative project which would be the first of its kind in the nation.

Homefulness, which is based in Deep East Oakland, includes four side-by-side straw-bale multi-family townhomes, community gardens, a school and a community center.

This extremely exciting project is led by a powerful collaboration of preeminent "natural" builders/architects, including Bob Theis, who was involved in the design and building of one of the first post-colonial straw-bale structures in Oakland, as well as youth and families who themselves have experienced homelessness, poverty, displacement, racism, immigration and eviction.

"The Homefulness project is working to make compact, ecological shelter available to the low-income city dwellers who need it most," said Theis.

The project has also been guided by First Nations Ohlone people of this land who are working on a self-determined land trust for this Ohlone territory, as well as by an innovative concept developed by POOR Magazine called Poverty Scholarship, i.e. the most impacted peoples should be leading and/or directly involved in their own, self-determined solutions.

"Homefulness was always the way of our African peoples, interdependence which we practice is a truly powerful way of taking care of Mama Earth and each other," said Queennandi Xsheba of POOR Magazine.

"Homefulness is a poor and indigenous people-led solution to Homelessness, it was conceived by my mother and me and several other homeless, disabled, and displaced community members while we were living in our car in Oakland, aware that our survival was linked to the survival not just of each other but to other people in homelessness and to Mama Earth," said Tiny Gray-Garcia, co-founder of POOR Magazine and author of the book Criminal of Poverty, Growing Up Homeless in America. Gray-Garcia continued, "In light of the recent

COP21 summit in Paris, it is more important than ever for cities like Oakland to take up visionary projects like Homefulness which work with Mother Earth's resources, not against her."

So far the planning department approved the Homefulness project, but the building department who grants the permits to begin the community-centered building project has had some trouble understanding this innovative and ancient vision to steward and care for Mama Earth and its people through age-old green materials.

"We hope the building department and the City of Oakland can see, with us, this powerful visionary way of taking care of Mama Earth through truly green, age-old natural building," said Miguel Soberanis, poverty and indigenous scholar with POOR Magazine.

What is the Stolen Land /Hoarded Resources Decolonization, Redistribution and Community Reparations Tour and the Bank of Community Reparations?

Herstory

The Stolen Land/Hoarded Resources tour launched on Mama Earth Day 2016 in the stolen Lisjen/Ohlone Village of Yelamu (SF) in CalifAztlan, with poor & indigenous peoples touring "rich" neighborhoods across the US and knocking on doors humbly asking that wealth hoarders redistribute their surplus money, resources and assets to poor and indigenous led land liberation movements. The tour has so far toured 8 wealth-hoarding cities across the US including Beverly Hills, San Francisco, Oakland, Manhattan, Conn and Philadelphia Poor & indigenous Tour Guides are joined by conscious folks with race and class privilege walking in solidarity and change.

The tour is loosely based on the Bhoodan Movement of India launched by Vinoba Bhave who walked through India asking wealthy "land-owners" to gift their land to landless peoples. With a similar vision, this small group of landless and indigenous peoples being hit the hardest by displacement and gentrification will be intentionally crossing the invisible and visible lines between the land and resource hoarders aka the very rich and the victims of generations of white supremacy, theft, colonization, criminalization, racism, eugenics and silencing, aka the very poor.

Two action models/solutions that Homeless and 1st Nations folks are presenting is the poor people-led self-determined movement called Homefulness in Deep East Oakland (Huchuin Ohlone Land) as well as Sogorea Te Land Trust which is a Native Woman run land trust based in the land of the 1st peoples who lead it.

The Bank of Community Reparations

This tour officially launches the **Bank of Community Reparations**—a national fund of redistributed and stolen wealth that is distributed equally among poor and indigenous people-led land use projects—the 1st four of which are the following:

1) **Homefulness in Deep East Huchuin(Oakland)**, a poor and indigenous-led landless peoples movement working to build 9 units of housing for unhoused families and elders, a liberation school, radio station, garden and healing center in Deep east Oakland

2) **Sogorea Te Land Trust** (Huchuin/Oakland) the first Native woman-run land trust working to reclaim stolen Ohlone/Lisjen land (Oakland)

3) **Homefulness #2/3/4 & Beyond**—Anywhere in Occupied, Colonized MamaEarth (Launched by fellow poverty skolaz in collaboration with Conscious "inheritors" of stolen wealth or land across Mama Earth

For more information on the Tour and/or Revolutionary Giving to the Bank of Reparations call (510) 435-7500 or email poormag@ gmail.com. To register for the next PeopleSkool Seminar for Folks with Race/Class Privilege email deeandtiny@gmail.com or go on-line to www.racepovertymediajustice.org or www.poormagazine.org

Stolen Land Tours

Stolen Land Tours through so-called Beverly Hills, so-called Cherry Creek, CO, Huchiun, Pomo Territory, tech gentrifiers in so-called San Francisco, so-called Olympia, and UC Hastings

Akkkademic Reparations on Stolen Land

Maya Ram

"We are at this place right now where we're doing land acknowledgements, but do we get to go to these institutions? Not ONE Lisjan person has been educated at UC Berkeley," said Corrina Gould at 'Degentrifying Academia from Huichin (Berkeley) to Lenape (Philly): Taking Back Land, Culture, and Ancestors' on April 28th. Corrina, spokesperson for the Confederated Villages of Lisjan/Ohlone and co-founder of Sogorea Te' Land Trust, talked about how buildings at UC Berkeley hoard remains of 9,000 stolen indigenous ancestors. Akkkademic institutions have the power to tell false, colonized histories—from UC Berkeley in the Bay Area to Temple University in Philly—as they sit on indigenous burial sites and village sites.

POOR Magazine—alongside comrades from Poor People's Army, #FreeKashmir, Sogorea Te' Land Trust, Krip Hop Nation, and many more Poverty Skolaz—shared powerful knowledge, WeSearch, questions and a demand for UC Berkeley in the last few weeks. A call for the end to hoarded wealth, stolen ancestors, and gentrifukation.

"As we talk about landless people's movements, it is vital that we open these conversations to Poverty Skolaz," said Lisa "Tiny" Gray-Garcia, co-founder of POOR Magazine and Homefulness. "Of the homeless people in Oakland, around 50% are Black, 30% are white, over 80% are disabled and many are elders—all because of this lie called 'crapitalism' and this lie called 'wealth.'" We see how akkkademia fuels crapitalism and wealth hoarding in the current actions of UC Berkeley. In People's Park & at 1921 Walnut St., UC Berkeley—which already owns 40% of land in Berkeley—is trying to evict disabled elders and displace houseless people (including students) to build dorms that will only house students who can pay. UC Berkeley chooses to line its own pockets at the expense of residents of People's Park & 1921 Walnut, and their own student body.

Stealing of indigenous land and displacing families and elders is reflected in struggles for liberation around the world. Huma Dar, a Kashmiri academic, activist & mama, notes that during a global pandemic, "Nomadic indigenous people and elders are being evicted from their homes in Kashmir." As wealthy, Hindu, caste-privileged citizens purchase stolen Kashmiri land, we see a mirrored displacement of poor and indigenous peoples. And circling back to Turtle Island: "West of Temple University was 96% black in 2000, but after gentrification in 2010 was about 50% white and college-age residents were ⅔ of the population," said Galen Tyler, an organizer in West Philly from Poor People's Army.

At the Stolen Land/Hoarded Resources Tour at UC Berkeley on May 5th, youth skolaz from Deecolonize Academy taught us that almost every building on campus is named after a eugenicist. Akkkademic institutions may not have a problem with placing a racist colonizer's name on a building, but people with akkkademic privilege—like students, professors, lecturers and community members—do. They used their collective power to partner with POOR Magazine for a Stolen Land Tour on their campus to learn about akkkademic reparations.

When I think about akkkademic reparations, I think about my mama. Growing up poor in India to parents who were farmers that migrated to the city, she was taught the colonial myth that akkkademia is what saves you, what gets you out of a bad place. If I knew one thing growing up, it was that I had to go to college in order to make it. My akkkademic access and class privilege brought me to college, all the way across the country, running from abuse and my family. In my pursuit of success, of making it on my own, of earning my own money and keeping myself afloat, I was never taught the true lie of these institutions. That they steal land and labor and people's homes and the bones of indigenous ancestors in order to make "dreams come true." The dream that was fed to me was never real...it was always an illusion. The illusion that hard work—instead of privilege—leads to success and money. That getting degrees makes me smarter or more worthy of some white dude's respect. That respectability is above respect for land, elders and ancestors.

Shattering this lie and seeing akkkademia for what it truly is was my first step in akkkademic reparations and getting in right relationship with the land I'm on and the people whose land I'm on. POOR

Magazine and PeopleSkool helped me get to a place where I could hold my family histories of power, privilege AND oppression with love and pain...knowing that the way forward is radically redistributing to follow the guidance of my poor ancestors.

It's like Leroy Moore of Krip Hop Nation said: "Poor people have the answers, and we cannot go back (to before Covid). We have an extraordinary opportunity to radically change things moving forward."

Stolen Land/Hoarded Resources, Ancestors, Land and Culture Back Demand for UC Berkeley

From POOR Magazine, Homefulness, Deecolonize Academy, Indians Organizing for Change and Krip Hop Nation.

DEMAND:

We the Indigenous, unHoused, Displaced, Privatized, Enslaved, Bordered, poLiced, Disabled, and profited off of Peoples Present to UC Berkeley a Demand of Land back for Evicted and Unhoused People, PoLice Harassed and gentriFUKed out for the Borm Industrial Complex and the land hoarding and resource theft perpetrated by institutions like UC Berkeley and UC Hastings.

We also offer to begin a dialogue with Academia to redistribute, reparate, and begin a generational and ancestral healing process from the disease of wealth and/or resource hoarding, generational or inherited land-stealing, displacing, academic or cultural theft, and/or desecrating of indigenous bodies, houseless bodies, Disabled bodies, Black and Brown and incarcerated and silenced Peoples.

We Demand Land Back and reparations for the Genrations of Cultural theft and Cultural appropriation of disabled black and brown and indigenous bodies and that People's Park and 1921 Walnut Street apartments remain intact, never displaced or threatened with removal again.

As well that houseless and indigenous people be supported with reparations and returned stolen resources and stolen "studied" knowledge so we can build our own solutions to our own problems informed by #PovertyScholarship like Homefulness and Deecolonize Academy.

A session of PeopleSkool at Poor Magazine is offered to the institution as part of this Healing—informed by Poverty Scholarship: Poor People-led Theory, Art, Words and Tears Across Mama Earth.

All the language in this article challenging linguistic domination is brought to you by Lisa "Tiny" Gray-Garcia & POOR Magazine... check out Poverty Scholarship *at poorpress.net for more on linguistic domination*

Youth Visions of Homefulness

Homefulness is like Heaven

Amir Cornish, DeeColonize Academy

Homefulness is a community launched by Dee and Tiny Garcia. Homefulness is a safe place for people of color that could join us in the movement to free Mama Earth along with all of our Po Uncles, Aunties, Grandmas and Grandpas. I study at Deecolonize Academy—a school at Homefulness in East Oakland.

Homefulness is a place that helps homeless people on the streets. We give out food to see their smiles. They also have their own radio show led by youth skolaz and adult skolaz. Also we support our people in the streets.

Homefulness is not just a place, it's much more than a place- it's like heaven. We save lives during this pandemic, we always help our community and never stop, always help the poor. Homefulness is a place where you can feel safe.

Homefulness is different from the other schools. It is led by our community from the streets. They are also teaching the young ones how to take care of the elders in our community. Homefulness teaches so many things that are different from the regular schools.

Homefulness is a special space for all of us and this community fights the cruel injustice on our people. We are not a fake organization. We are the real deal, and we are always showing up and supporting anyone who needs our help.

Rags To Rooms: Deecolonize Academy Final Essay 2020

Kimo Umo

In my life, I've been asked to remember my experience of being formerly homeless. To be honest, there have been times I've forgotten about this fact, a truth I struggle to cope with. With a society like the United States, we Americans tend to glamorize certain aspects like being rich over being poor.

In my earlier years of living in the Bay Area, I was at the age of 6 when I was homeless on the streets of San Francisco. My mom, Linda, who was in her mid 30s, had been going through what she describes as "the hardest time of her life." She had just herself and I enrolled into a homeless shelter, called the Hamilton.

My mother had lived in actual shelters for 6 months while I lived with my grandpa in Stockton. This was dangerous because of the distribution of narcotics and actions more devious than the devil. After the 6 months were up, my mom got a house in Oakland and I moved back in. She also had a new boyfriend, Carlos, who helped financially but that still wasn't enough to stop us from getting evicted from Oakland.

Since I was a toddler at the time, my day consisted of waking up at 6:00AM, getting my bag ready, empty of any school supplies, and having a golden peanut butter sandwich. This sandwich was better than the ham sandwich, which was the opposite of sweet and being cold as a rock. Even though I didn't like the sandwiches all the time, it was better than starving.

My life was like this for the next year. From 2007 to 2009, my mom struggled to find housing but eventually struck gold and was able to get into a program that helps families in homeless shelters get access to public housing. For example, my mother and I ended up getting a house in one of San Francisco's ghettos known as Hunter's Point.

On January 29, 2008 while at the shelter, my mom and I were waiting for one of the staff. We had been accepted into the public housing projects in the southeast end of the city. It seemed like my mom and I were preparing for a covert mission, preparing gear in the night with wool blankets and clothes.

We all gathered our things together and proceeded into the van. We were accompanied by multiple families who were just as traumatized as the other people. Like midnight riders, the rubber hit the road and people were getting dropped off to their own luxury neighborhoods and projects.

Oddly enough, all these people were just like mom and I. They didn't have a place to go until now. Maybe they were somewhat abandoned by someone too. It's hard to believe there were so many people who had the same predicament as me. And yet I was off to my own home, as my mom put it "We had just won the lottery ticket." The struggling had paid off finally.

When the van arrived at its destination, mom and I were out of the van swiftly. We were off on our own voyage and it felt refreshing as if we were unloading into a new country like Cuba. It was like a big container ship disembarking from a long time at sea. When sailors are adrift for long periods of time, one may begin to miss the land back home.

The house was a two story building. It was conjoined with another house as if stacked on top of each other, as if they were stairs. My mom couldn't be happier. We arrived at the house and were hastily able to get some sleep. The shelter did not provide beds for our new home, so we just slept on the blankets. It was the safest I had felt in awhile and I bet it was for my mom too.

I slept so soundly that night not even the bang of a stick of dynamite could wake me. The next morning I awoke to a bright warm yellow morning of English muffins and peanut butter. My first bite of the food was gooey but delicious. I even met some of my first friends at a bus stop nearby. A little white boy with his mom just like me said hello and turned out to be my neighbor.

The next 11 years I still feel the effects of my past and how I survived because of my mother's determination to not be raised in her hometown of Stockton. She says boys my age die of common causes like being entangled with gangs or drugs. Those aspects are still around me in Hunter's Point, but it's tamer.

Life for now is about trying to better myself and those around me. It usually starts with yourself. Remembering being homeless makes me humble. Not that I liked being homeless. But I do understand it's hard and it can be a death sentence.

Homefulness #2

A Formerly Houseless child helps to build the future—I am Tiburcio Garcia, a formerly homeless youth who goes to school at Deecolonize Academy. I am someone who is able to gaze along the spectrum of class, walking a fine line between privilege and poverty. I have privilege in so many ways: a loving, kind, mother who constantly supports and educates me, a community to lift me up immediately when I fall, friends who have my back, and a healthy relationship which on my part is due to the mannerly way I was raised. However, in the eyes of this government and many others, I am seen as someone with hardly iaiaiaiaiaiaiaiaiaiaiaiaiaiaiaiaiaiaiaiaiaiaiaiaiaiaiaiaiaiaiaiaiaiaiaiaiaiaiaiaiaiaiaiaiaiaiaiaiaiaia ia ia iaiaiaiaiaiaiaiaia ia ia iaia ia ia ia ia ia ia ia ia ia ia ia ia ia ia ia ia ia ia ia ia ia iaia ia ia ia ia ia ia ia iaia ia

anything, struggling to survive. That's why the project that was started by my mother, grandmother and everyone else at POOR Magazine is so important to me. That project is called Homefulness, and it's what's making sure me and my mother aren't homeless to this day.

Homefulness is a poor people's solution to homelessness, and we are starting another one. July 21, a day that is divisible by 3, was the day that we decided to start on the second version based off of the template of the original Homefulness, only two blocks down. I can still feel the grass snaking around my ankle and the weeds and vines getting stuck to my gloves. The air was saturated with pollen, and the sounds of weed whackers in the background were blending with the noise of cars passing by and multiple conversations. After a couple of minutes of hard work, pulling up grass and snipping particularly vicious fennel, I started to feel the sweat from my hair run down my back, and the hairs on my arm crisping. It was a "I need water right now even though I had a cup 5 minutes ago" day, and all of the students of the summer camp we were attending were working hard next to other residents of Homefulness and members of POOR Magazine.

This land that Homefulness resides on isn't an ordinary plot, and those weeds that we were cutting were going to disappear eventually because without our intervention that innocent half-pavement, half overgrown lot would have spelled doom for our community. We originally found out about this land while doing our Hoarded Mama Earth and Community Reparations research, and we later found out that land would have become 20 luxury condominiums, bringing in a hoard of gentrifiers that would have completely changed the ecosystem of this environment, just like it did in the city I was born and raised in, San Francisco, and eventually had to move out of due to eviction caused by that gentrification.

I am formerly houseless, and in the eyes of the system, I am not privileged in the slightest. I don't see that. I know I am one of the most privileged people on this planet, because I actually get to shape history as it progresses. I am young, but I get to be a part of a project that will house thousands of families just like mine all over the world one day. On that day July 21, I got to lay the groundwork for Homefulness 2, the second homeless people's solution to homelessness that will very well house and give privilege to kids just like it did for me.

Tiburcio Garcia

My name is Ziair and as I walk on the campus and get ready for summer camp at Deecolonize Academy, I sit down and eat. Then we did martial arts with Brother Mink.

Afterwards we all sat down and talked about how we're gonna go to Homefulness 2. When we got there we prayed. Everybody had goggles, shields and gloves. We brought trash bags, rakes and weed cutters. We paired up into teams and got the garbage from off the site. We also cut the weeds.

We were cleaning up the site. There was a lot of shattered glass and old glass bottles, and the land looked like a jungle. We chopped all the weeds, cut and rake the grass, then took a break for the interview for the show about what we were doing. Everyone was hot and sweaty. But there was a goal we got it done because it was important. We got there at 11am and ended at 12pm.

Cleaning up is fun and pretty good exercise. Starting at Homefulness #1, which we are still trying to build as poor and houseless peoples, to then make Homefulness #2 happen is a big Journey. But with all our family we made it happen and are liberating another small part of land.

Us all being homeless we never had a home that was stable or a place we could go to count on, so that's why we're providing it for the homeless now. Because we knew how it felt to not have anyone to lean on and have no support.

in conclusion: as we closed out the land, it looks better already. We shared our thoughts about what we did and then prayed. It was very needed that we did all that stuff, so that we can take care of our land and not junk It up. I'm glad I was able to help out.

Ziair Hughes

The youth did WeSearch about the vacant lots that were empty for days, maybe months. The youth skolas called the owners of the vacant lots. And Decolonize got one of the vacant lots and is building another Homefulness.

I am Amir Cornish. I'm a student of Deecolonize Academy, and we are a group that helps the community. I live in West Oakland.

Homefulness 2 is the same as Homefulness, and Poor Magazine created the first Homefulness ever. But Homefulness 2 is another extension for Poor Magazine. They're both in East Oakland.

Homefulness 2 is going to be a wonderful place for a community and we hope this Homefulnes 2 will grow into the world and also bring all the community people together as a unit, to finally unsell mama earth around the world.

Homefulness 2 is a start for the community because we could tell the world we finally made it by ourselves and say we don't need the government or gentrifiers that are breaking our community apart.

Homefulnews 2 is a work in progress. The youth, adults and elders helped clean the Homefulness 2 place up, but this is a community that builds nothing into something also nobody can really do that.

Amir Cornish

RAD & Gentrifukation in San Francisco
by Jack Minel

2009 was the year my mom and I were no longer homeless in San Francisco, due to the tenacity of my mother, Linda Montoya, and pure luck. My mom spent her efforts filing applications when I was homeless with her in a shelter, known as the Hamilton. She filed a Section 8 paper, which allowed certain low-income families—when certified by local house ambassadors—to be allowed to rent a private property.

My mom and I were certainly gifted by fate. We were able to shelter before the new ongoing wave of gentrification that flooded the city in a matter of years. Since it was 2009, there were many people moving out of their low-income housing units as well as coming in to renovate. Our only form of income at the time was the Social Security check she would get, which I assume was nearly $900. Our rent was $200 a month from the beginning, plus electricity, etc.

Fast forward 12 years later. Now, I live on 25 Northridge Road, located on the southern eastern end of San Francisco. The hills are steep and they make bones brittle faster than when you mush styrofoam packaging. My mom and I are familiar with the terrain which we live upon. The hills are steep and my mother is growing older in age, getting into her 50s now. Even I have a hard time getting up the stairs during grocery runs to the store.

Even though these things are tough, to stand aside and let the threat of gentrification continue is something I can't do. I have gone through most of the phases of the RAD reconstruction of my neighborhood of Hunter's Point, and with some quick fact checking, I also see there are many other chapters buying low-income housing for the purpose of conversions.

The conversion of the houses around me are nice, but I can't help but get the feeling this is just the calm before the storm. San Francisco is going through a change from the grassroots culture it's known for. It's turning and transforming into a city of technology as well as a high influx of foreign residency, known as the "techies."

Many friends and families have been drowned out with gentrification and swept from their homes. And I fear that time is coming for my mom and I. Through gaining confidence in a new found perspective, it's time to speak up and fight against the terror of gentrification.

If we can come together, we just might have the momentum to sway the odds in the people's favor.

Encampment Bans

It is difficult to find information on encampment bans in California. I believe this isn't an accident, because these "bans" against the safe gathering of people who have nowhere else to go is the ugly side of our state. A side they aren't so eager to make public to the world. When I search the topic, I am purposely shown stories of how the "homeless problem" has terrorized San Francisco and the Bay Area for decades as well as how previous and current mayors have helped the homeless. MIllions of dollars, task forces, temporary shelters, and kkkages designed to imprison our people without saying it out loud. These strategies have been used to solve the homeless problem. However, we aren't a problem or a solution that needs to be fixed. That, however, is the gaze that dominates most mainstream media, and because of that, Oakland's new Encampment Management Policy is receiving widespread support.

"It's not a really well thought out plan, it's redlining," said a lady from the Wood St. houseless encampment when asked about this new initiative created and led by the City of Oakland. "The H word (referring to the word 'homeless') is the new N-word," she continued.

This lady, who had lived in this area for 8 years after being burned out of her previous occupation, let it be known that she has nowhere to go if this plan is put in place. Deecolonize Academy went to the encampment after hearing there was going to be a mass displacement. We went there to hear more about what was going on from the source. We learned that a billionaire by the name of Fred B. Craves, who owns a fish oil distribution company, is attempting to displace all of the houseless people from his portion of stolen Huichin land.

This new Encampment Management Policy is actually a few key plans grouped together called PATH. The PATH framework includes prevention, protection, emergency response, and housing development. Protection means protection for low-income people from losing their housing and becoming houseless, with a subtext stating that "prevention strategies aren't addressed in this policy." This statement makes the first strategy a lie among many that these Policies and Bans present to the public. Emergency response means sheltering and rehousing,

including building houses for houseless people. However, it is only for the ones who qualify and go through years of paperwork and waiting. And finally, housing development which is building new apartments and developing on more Indigenous land, instead of buying up and using the thousands of privately owned lots and abandoned houses that are all over the Bay Area.

"This Encampment Management Policy is a bunch of bull****. It's really a codification of what the City of Oakland has been doing forever. Now they're just putting it in the books so they can eventually displace all working people in Oakland," states Dale, representing the United Front Against Displacement, when asked about the aforementioned Policy. He continued, "...all the people experiencing homelessness, even who might be housed right now, are under threat of being completely displaced from Oakland."

While researching the history of encampment bans in San Francisco and the Bay Area, a couple of things stood out to me. I see amazing, inspiring photos, first black and white but as the years became more recent, with color, of our former mayors: Feinstein, Browi, Newsom, Lee, and then our current mayor, London Breed. All of those pictures are the same but also different. The mayor is standing with the homeless people or holding some kind of cleaning or construction tool showing that they do so much for the homeless. All the while, they are ordering the Department of Public Works to sweep the very people they were just "talking to."

For example, Feinstein relied on church shelters to take care of the "problem." Brown declared that homelessness was a problem that "may not be solvable." Newsom, with his "Care not Cash" program, slashed cash payments to houseless people and instead focused on housing that only helped a small percentage of people and charred them for shelter beds. Lee cleared large swatches of SoMa (South of Market) to appease the massive wave of tech gentrification. Breed is currently driving a "housing first" initiative, safe RV lots, and safe injection sites while she continues the DPW sweeps and creates a 30% increase of the houseless population since 2017. With Oakland's new Encampment Management Policy, we are going to see the same things happen as they have in the history of the Bay Area—the continual forceful removal of people who have nowhere else to go and are just trying to survive.

Tiburcio Garcia

Sweeping Signatures—I dream of the days where I will be writing about all the good news that is yet to come. When the headlines are "Poverty has ended!" "Racism is no more!" But here I am, writing about another policy passed to oppress the poor even more. This new policy is called the "Encampment Management Policy." The policy bans tents from being within 150 feet of schools and 50 feet from homes, businesses, playgrounds, parks, and other recreation areas.

City Councilman Noel Gallo said that he is frustrated by the camps, tents, and trash. His solution to it is to move it all out of sight. This doesn't really solve anything. It just allows more sweeps and restrictions to homelessness. Dale, from the United Front Against Displacement, said the policy "doesn't actually do anything to address the needs people have because that's not what it's intended to do."

Deecolonize Academy went to visit an encampment at Wood Street in Oakland. This lot had been receiving a lot of harassment, officially and unofficially. They had received eviction notices and also secret police raids. The lot is owned by wealth hoarder Fred B. Craves who got a lot of his money by finding new ways to produce fish oil. He had said that he wanted to turn the lot into a safe RV lot. But after watching the construction workers mark the ground and doing some additional research, it turns out that he wants to turn it into a research facility. The marks the construction workers made implied a whole building was going to be built instead of just providing resources for an RV lot.

RV lots aren't a solution anyway. There is an RV lot close to this encampment at 34th and Wood St. but it's not any better. People there get served spoiled food. The porta potties are not maintained. They have restrictions on what people can bring into the lot. And they have a curfew. In fact, the gate is locked between 4pm-10am, making the RV lot a cage.

This new policy is another attack on people in struggle. Laws won't be on our side as long as colonizers, wealth hoarders, politricksters, and Klan members rule this system. We aren't represented in this system and it's something that has to change. Policies and laws clearly aren't made to help, they just solidify the power that the colonizers already have. A person has to create their own solutions, not wait for others to give them to you.

Akil Carrillo

On October 13, 2020, we arrived at the encampment in West Oakland ready to take notes. The place was trashy because of the police moving homeless people's belongings everywhere. Then instantly we ran into a member of the United Front Against Displacement—Dale. He said, "We work primarily with the Wood Street Homeless community." But in general, they are a community organization building solidarity between working class folks and houseless folks. They work to prevent homeless people from experiencing criminalization or displacement from the state.

The owner of the lot, Fred Beraves, is a billionaire. He made his money finding a new way to produce fish oil. The reason he made his company, Game Changer LLC, was to buy up "real estate" to develop it and make more money. He's planning to turn the lot into a biomedical technical research facility so he can make millions. "He said that he wanted to turn it into a safe RV lot, but there is no document that says he's doing that," said Dale.

Then we talked to a community member and they said that it is not a fully thought out plan. "It's red lining, it is the n word." The system is telling people they "can't be by the park, can't be by the school, can't be by the store," they concluded. This person has been there 8 years. They've negotiated with the rails to stay there, on the other side of the fence because they felt safer there.

This citizen added, "I'm still kind of green when it comes to being homeless." I learned that the houseless folks could stay until they got their house back, which had been taken from them. They added, "There is still no law or law groups that are addressing the fact that one third of our population has their homes taken from them by relatives."

Ziair Hughes

Homefulness Mural Unveiling

Chapter 3
Poverty Skolaz' Stories & Poems

Evicting Elders

Eviction is Elder Abuse—A Youth Skola Report

Eviction killed 100-year-old Iris Canada for a house she called home for 60 years. She was a Black elder who raised children in the home. Peter Owens, the landlord, was trying to flip it into a condo. Ms. Canada tried to fight her hardest to keep that house.

The planning commission rejected Peter Owens when he attempted to turn her house into a Condo. It is wrong that they're kicking out elders. If this was my granny, I would have a problem too if she was treated that way.

Ziair Hughes

The Ellis Act is a state law which says that landlords have the unconditional right to evict tenants to "go out of business." This landlord-written law has been used to enable speculators to buy apartment buildings filled with long-term tenants and "legally evict" all the tenants living there so that after a short wait, they can re-rent all the vacant units for any insane price they want.

Eviction is elder abuse. POOR Magazine did precedent-setting work naming that Ellis Act evictions of elders are elder abuse under 368 code:

"Any person who knows or reasonably should know that a person is an elder or dependent adult and who, under circumstances or conditions likely to produce great bodily harm or death, willfully causes or permits any elder or dependent adult to suffer, or inflicts thereon unjustifiable physical pain or mental suffering, or having the care or custody of any elder or dependent adult, willfully causes or permits the person or health of the elder or dependent adult to be injured, or willfully causes or permits the elder or dependent adult to be placed in a situation in which his or her person or health is endangered, is punishable by imprisonment in a county jail not exceeding one year, or by a fine not to exceed six thousand dollars ($6,000), or by both that fine and

imprisonment, or by imprisonment in the state prison for two,
three, or four years."

Eviction is elder abuse and yet we still accept laws that kick out our elders who are 60 years or older. It's a shame that a city like San Francisco says it wants to take care of its residents but landowners have the audacity to kick out a 99-year-old woman, like Iris Canada, onto the streets. Eviction causes anxiety and pain for our elders. Elders get ill and sometimes die from the stress because it's too much to bear at one time.

Evictions are a problem for everyone. It's like a cycle of life. It happens so much we get used to hearing our communities getting kicked out of their homes because of poverty and the struggle people with a welfare check face every month.

In the end, we poverty scholars understand that we need elders so they remind us of the mistakes of the past and help guide the future of our children.

Kimo Umu

RAD Public Housing Privatization—Stealing Our Last Acre and Our One Remaining Mule

Tiny AKA Lisa Gray-Garcia
September 23, 2013, Reprinted With
Permission from the *SF Bay View*

"Can you guarantee there will be housing for low, low income people, cause many of our folks are low, low income?" the inquiry from SF Public Housing Commissioner Patricia Thomas was tentative, her voice building power with each word.

"RAD is an integrated model that preserves affordable housing," replied Olson Lee in a careful monotone, representative of the Mayor's office of Housing.

"Mr. Lee, you are not answering my question, is the Mayor's office guaranteeing that there will be housing for low, low-income people, or like one of the public commenters said, we will we be gentrified out of our own communities?"

New-Orleans-public-housing-demolition, RAD public housing privatization: Stealing our last acre and our one remaining mule, Local News & Views

The San Francisco Housing Commission meeting of September 4th on a new acronym called Rental Assistance Demonstration (RAD), code for selling public housing to private investors, was still. Still like a grave. A grave for all us poor peoples' destruction from the massive privatization of our public housing. Us unprioritized and barely housed, the holding-on-by-our-fingernails-families, the forgotten elders, the un-remembered disabled folks, the very poor, the displaced, now houseless and rarely remembered.

I was the public commenter Ms. Thomas referenced who brought the deadly "G" word (Gentrification – or what we at POOR affection-ately call GentriFUKation) into the tomb-like room. After listening to an onslaught of thinly veiled lies presented by the Mayors Office of Housing (MOH), cloaked in feel-good titles like SFHA Re-visioning, projected onto PowerPoint presentations using confusing terms like outcomes and clusters, and littered with acronyms, my body was shaking with fury and betrayal. Sadly, this was nothing new. POOR Magazine poverty skolaz have been writing, WeSearching and protesting this mess since our inception. There was just a deeper arrogance about the theft than we have seen before.

"He (Olson Lee) can't guarantee it. They are selling public housing stocks off to private investors as mortgages, so of course they can't guarantee what private investors do with their investments," said Paul Boden. I called Paul from Western Regional Advocacy Project (WRAP), who has done extensive research on the destruction of public housing for poor peoples in the US, to get some truth beyond the acronyms.

One of the statements that is continually used by politricksters about public housing is the "obvious need for a solution to the problem of public housing." The truth is, according to (WRAP)'s Without Housing report, beginning as far back as the 1960's when President Nixon put a federal moratorium on the building of HUD's afford-able housing (aka poor people housing) the government sponsored gentriFUKation plans have been rolling out one brutal slice at a time, making sure that the New Deal idea of public housing for all became a "failure."

Throw in rampant re-devilment across the nation that has hit the Black community more deeply than any other folks, the implementation of the paper-based mythology of the Section 8 program which has never been a guarantee to housing and has already lost over 300,000 units to foreclosure and opt-outs since the 90's, and is currently barely surviving the so-called sequester hits, combined with the demolition of over 200,000 units of public housing, you have a planned government-baked recipe for the end of public housing.

Shuttled in with the benign title of Rental Assistance Development or acronym of RAD, a series of last minute, so-called "community" meetings are being held in the public housing projects that will be bought and sold right under us, claiming they will be improving our lives and communities by displacing us, just like every redevil-opment project has done since its inception such as Fill-no-more/Western Addition in San Francisco to the Brooklyn gentriFUKation of the 70's to Phoenix, Arizona's Joe Arpaio-funded destruction of poor people hotels downtown in the 90's to almost any city you can name in Amerikkka.

But the reality is, the devil-opers are running out of communities to gentriFUK so the next frontier is turning all of our public housing into private so-called "affordable" housing, with the complicit involvement of corporate government forces like the Jerry Brown, Gavin Newsom, Lee, Jean Quan, Villagarosa, Michael Bloomberg, administrations of San Francisco, Oakland, LA, New York and beyond.

"In the last four months, over a hundred representatives from 72 different organizations including residents, non-profit service providers, affordable housing developers, local labor unions and private sector development experts along with 20 city departments and representatives from HUD have met a total of 18 times."

— SFHA REVISIONING PROCESS RECOMMENDATIONS

"We have had multiple meetings in the communities leading up to this application," said Naomi Kelly, Mayors Office of Housing representative.

That's funny, I thought, neither myself nor any of our POOR Magazine family who are currently living in public housing units have got notices of these so-called tenant meetings, or any meetings about this for that matter.

The City of San Francisco has a deadline of September 30th to "apply" for RAD and we are all caught up in a wave we barely understand. This false urgency set by politricknologists have launched a whole slew of meetings scheduled with little or no notice ensuring that hardly any poor, disabled, elder, or working folks can make it to them. This take-down in the night is also possible cause so many of our backs, souls, and spirits are broken by years of race and poverty hits, Post-traumatic slave syndrome and the lie of capitalism in Amerikkka.

The other glaringly obvious part of these private devil-opments is their colonizer work crews who are flown in like the 21st century carpetbaggers they are to "work" on the construction sites.

"These developments are in our communities, why aren't they hiring us in the community," said Fly Benzo, Hip Hop Youth Skola, Media producer, and revolutionary Bayview son of Claude Carpenter, a leader in the building trades based in the Bay View. Fly, Claude,

Mary, and Willie Ratcliff and many others have been speaking truth to this colonizer situation for years, and yet the construction bids keep magically going to anyone but local folks. (Fly's powerful statements were caught in the new movie, Let em Hear Ya Comin, by revolutionary comrades Black Riders Liberation Party.)

"My family has been living in the Fillmore public housing projects for over 5 generations, where is our equity?" said Queennandi XSheba, fellow poverty skola reporter, poet, and welfareQUEEN at POOR Magazine.

In the end it is up to us family, to take back our 1/16th of an acre and half of a hoof of a mule. Like Queennandi, so many of us have lived in these devil-oped and intentionally destroyed communities so long, po'lice harassed, contained, redlined, gentriFUKed, under-employed, incarcerated, and never respected and yet as my strong black/Indian Mama Dee would always say, "What do we have to show for it?"

This is why us Po' folks/evicted, landless/houseless peoples (some of us living in so-called "public housing") at POOR Magazine launched the Homefulness project. Un-philathro-pimped and never devil-oper controlled, it puts the equity, decisions, power in the hands of all us peoples who are usually only told what and where we can go and do.

We have a 10-point plan to teach/share with any and all public housing tenants who want to fight for their own control. You have equity, you have the ability to stop this take-down and take back your own stolen resources, rooted in thousands of plantation lies that go back into generations of Amerikkklan/Colonizer lies.

The Crime of Ellis Act Evictions: The people charge landlords with elder abuse for Ellis Act evictions

Tiny, aka Lisa Gray-Garcia, daughter of Dee, mama of Tiburcio
February 11, 2014, *SF Bay View*

On Wednesday, Feb. 5 citing California Penal Code Section 368, we, the evicted, gentrified, policed, elderly, and disabled, walked into the Hall of Justice in San Francisco to bring criminal charges of elder abuse against landlords for the perpetration of the crime of Ellis Act evictions against frail, elder, disabled, and traumatized residents of San Francisco.

Remigio Fraga, elder activist with the Idriss Stelley Foundation, a co-sponsor of this action, makes the message clear outside the Hall of Justice. Photo: Poor News Network

Becoming homeless as an already disabled senior almost killed me," said Kathy Galvez, African descendent elder. She was evicted in 2012 from her San Francisco home of 40 years so that a realtor and bank gangster could profit from her now stolen home.

Due to the predatory speculation of landlords like Urban Green and lawyers like Andrew Sacks trying to scramble to make profit from the huge influx of new tech employees flooding the Bay Area, thousands of families with young children and disabled elders have been served with Ellis Act eviction notices. Or, they have already been evicted, ending up in the streets, in shelters, or most terrifying of all, dead from the trauma of eviction and homelessness.

The Ellis Act is a state law which says that landlords have the unconditional right to evict tenants to "go out of business." This landlord-written law has been used to enable speculators to buy apartment buildings filled with long-term tenants and "legally evict" all the tenants living there. Then, after a short wait, they re-rent all the vacant units for any insane price they want.

"I have nowhere to go."

Pictures of Black Herstory filled every inch of Miss Nan's walls. Mamas, daughters, sons, uncles, aunties, grandmamas, and great-greats looked down at me as Miss Nan spoke. "This whole eviction process has made me extremely ill. I was already sick, but I'm not sure if I'm going to make it now," she said.

The voice of 75-year-old Miss Nan was shaking as she spoke about the Ellis Act eviction notice she and her neighbors had just received. This would mean she, an African American disabled elder and life-long resident of San Francisco, will be evicted from her home of 43 years. "I have nowhere to go, and I can hardly walk. And now they are sending people out here to harass me," she concluded.

POOR Magazine's co-editor and Manilatown son, Tony Robles, and I were there sitting in her humble living room with Judge Judy quietly adjudicating on the old school Panasonic in the background, trying desperately to "save" Miss Nan from the vicious crime of eviction for profit.

As Miss Nan spoke, telling her story and the stories of her two disabled neighbors, one of whom had just been rushed to the hospital because he was so traumatized by receiving an Ellis Act eviction notice, her voice remained deep and strong. She was holding onto over 50 years of rent and bills paid, jobs tirelessly labored, unions joined, children born, families raised, elders cared for, and mamas transitioned. "I have nowhere to go," she repeated.

After holding the disgusting crime of Miss Nan's eviction on my heart, I was thrown back to the trauma of nine years ago. That was when me and my mama were given an Ellis Act eviction notice. It was the last straw, she said, after an already too long life of poverty and suffering, and the reason she became very sick and transitioned soon after.

Thousands of families with young children and disabled elders have been served with Ellis Act eviction notices, or have already been evicted, ending up in the streets, in shelters or, most terrifying of all, dead from the trauma of eviction and homelessness.

I remembered the family of Gerry Ambrose, a four generation working-class family dismantled by an Ellis Act eviction and eventual displacement to a trailer park in West Sacramento to the predatory impact of the first dot-com boom. That was my own eviction in 2010 under the Ellis Act of Mamahouse, a home for poor single parents like myself that I started in 2007.

And now Miss Nan, Benito Santiago, the entire block just Ellis Acted last month in North Beach, and dozens more. We at POOR Magazine have gotten calls every week for the last eight months and literally thousands more across the state of California, being evicted for profit of the few and the suffering of so many.

As a caregiver for elders, an advocate for all poor peoples who like myself and my family have struggled to survive in the inhuman system they call capitalism, and a good Indigenous daughter who has always practiced eldership, I realized then that these evictions under the Ellis Act, used for the profit of a few and causing the suffering of so many, were an actual crime, a crime of elder abuse.

The Filing

"I'm sorry, we can't take this complaint. You will need to go downstairs to the police window." When we first presented the detailed complaints of 12 disabled elders ranging in age from 62 to 95 years old, whose lives had been dismantled by the abuse of an Ellis Act eviction, the DA tried to give us what us po' folks call the "welfare shuffle"—sorry we can't help you, you need to go somewhere else.

But this time, for one of the few times in our unprotected and system-abused lives, someone stood up for our fight for the most unprotected in our society.

"Actually, no, this is the right place for us to be. Due to the enormity and seriousness of these charges, they have the right to go directly to the District Attorney," said Tony Prince, revolutionary lawyer who showed up for us and is also acting as Luis Rodriguez' campaign manager in his run for governor of California.

And then suddenly, almost as quickly as the "no" came out of her mouth, the DA's representative agreed to go to the back and consult with other attorneys. When she came back, she agreed to take our first seven complaints and make an appointment to sit down with us to discuss investigating them further.

Her "no" was not unexpected for us. Us poor and profiled folks of color have been told "no" more than we would care to count. Our lives and the lives of our young Black and Brown people are constantly arrested, cited, incarcerated, and harassed for less than what these landlords and speculators have gotten away with.

We are constantly called criminals and thugs and perpetrators and dangerous. And yet, who among us is abusing the most vulnerable of us? Who among us is creating sit-lie, stop and frisk, and gang injunction laws daily to keep our poor bodies constantly under threat and attack?

"We will be investigating any clear acts of elder abuse," said George Gascon to reporters who questioned him on our complaints.

"We need to put an end to the Ellis Act and other laws like it which cause more poverty and homelessness," said Luis Rodriguez, candidate for governor of California, who spoke at the press conference that preceded the filing.

The ultimate irony of capitalist defined crimes is who is considered the good, honest working people and who is considered the dangerous criminals? It is not our houseless peoples or Black and Brown young people who are throwing 95-year-old elders on the street in the cold with nowhere to go.

It is the people who have stolen this Indigenous land, charged us rent for it, and used papers and lawyers to destroy us. Those are the real criminals, the dangerous ones. They are the ones we need to watch out for. They are the ones who need to be cleaned off our streets and out of our neighborhoods before they abuse any more of us.

California Penal Code Section 368 (Elder Abuse Law)

"Any person who knows or reasonably should know that a person is an elder or dependent adult and who, under circumstances or conditions likely to produce great bodily harm or death, willfully causes or permits any elder or dependent adult to suffer, or inflicts thereon unjustifiable physical pain or mental suffering, or having the care or custody of any elder or dependent adult, willfully causes or permits the person or health of the elder or dependent adult to be injured, or willfully causes or permits the elder or dependent adult to be placed in a situation in which his or her person or health is endangered, is punishable by imprisonment in a county jail not exceeding one year, or by a fine not to exceed six thousand dollars ($6,000), or by both that fine and imprisonment, or by imprisonment in the state prison for two, three, or four years."

Join POOR to discuss elder abuse charges with the DA

This Friday, Feb. 14 at 12 noon, elders, families, and advocates will come back to 850 Bryant St. in San Francisco to hold a press conference on the front steps of the Hall of Justice. Then we will meet with the DA to pursue these criminal charges of elder abuse. Come join us.

Iris Canada turns 100 as her landlord tries to evict her

Tony Robles
July 10, 2016, 48Hills.org

A century of life—celebrated by a fight for her home. Is this elder abuse? Iris Canada turns 100 on July 13. Iris Canada, eviction fighter, who has lived in San Francisco's Black community on Page Street since the 1940s. Iris, with history in her skin and stories welling up in her eyes. The trees outside her home bend to the left and right, seeking balance in anticipation of her 100 years. It is more important than the Golden Gate Bridge and all the gold dust fairy tales peddled by get-rich con men and their schemes to pull the rugs and chairs out from under us. It is more important than Google, tech shuttles, cable cars, and the box of Rice-a-Roni.

Iris Canada sits with supporters outside a courtroom
where she fought her eviction

Iris speaks softly, so soft that you must listen carefully or you will miss what is important. Her voice is a caress of butter on a warm slice of toast in a kitchen whose walls breathe stories:

I was born in 1916, the same year the 19th Amendment gave women the right to vote. When I was 13, the stock market crashed. At 25, I cried with my country when Pearl Harbor was bombed and I celebrated with my country when the war ended. I was 38 when Brown vs. Board of Education ended segregation in American schools. At the age of 53, I felt old, having endured six of the worst years our country had ever seen as its leaders were murdered: Fred Hampton, Bobby Kennedy, Martin Luther King Jr., Malcolm X, John F. Kennedy, and Medgar Evers were assassinated from 1963-69. I lived through Watergate, the oil crisis, Iran Contra, and the assassination of Harvey Milk when I was 62. When I was 74 and had been collecting Social Security for 10 years, the US was fighting the Gulf War. I was so proud that I voted to elect our first African American president after my 92nd birthday.

In three days Iris turns 100. Did you expect to live this long? Did you imagine bearing witness to the Black community's population dwindling to 3% of the population of San Francisco? In your dreams, did you think that your building would be sold and that you would have to endure an Ellis Act eviction whose sole aim was to extricate you from your home? Iris, with a voice so soft—tell me.

I have lived and continue to live a rich and full life. I have paid my taxes, worked to improve the health and life of families and community members in neighborhoods locally. I have paid my dues. I am entitled to all the protections the laws allow for tenants and the elderly in the city of San Francisco. I am entitled to the quiet use and enjoyment of my home according to the protections of the state of California, from harassment and disenfranchisement due to the greed of property speculators and landlords involved in the race to take over all viable space in San Francisco for personal gain for the highly privileged. I have been under siege, harassed continually by my own neighbors, attacked in my own home, and fooled when I was well into my 80s into signing documents that did not benefit me by people who falsely claim to have my best interests at heart.

Iris Canada, part of the great migration of Black folks to San Francisco. She first lived on the 800th block of Page Street. Then she moved to her current home at 670 Page, where she has lived since the 1950s with her husband James. James was a deep sea diver in the military and later employed by United Airlines until his passing in the 1980s. Iris' home was a home. The original landlord, James Stephens, was a "gentleman who kept his word and realized his decisions affected the quality of life of his tenants."

Iris kept up the small garden whose bounty was shared among the tenants and Mr. Stephens. This was before sharing became known as tenancies in common (TICs).

When Mr. Stephens died, the building was sold to the current owner, Peter Owens, who, with his wife and brother, co-own Iris' building. They invoked the Ellis Act to evict her. She fought to stay in her home but the fight has resulted in her failing health, including hospital stays. Iris' landlords and neighbors want to convert the building into condos. Iris refused to sign paperwork allowing them to do so. In response, the neighbors have made Iris' living situation less than comfortable.

In three days, Iris turns 100.

Iris, we honor and celebrate your life. Thank you for being here. Thank you for staying on that block. Your presence brings us hope and pride. Your presence runs deeper than the tourist landmarks that are flat postcard images when compared to the fullness of your life. Compared to you, the Transamerica building is a dunce cap, Coit Tower a crushed cigarette butt. Attempts have been made to remove you from your home. It has caused tremendous stress on your 99-year-old body. Is this a birthday celebration or is it elder abuse?

California Pen Code 368 (Elder Abuse Law)
Any person who knows or reasonably should know that a person is an elder or dependent adult and who, under circumstances or conditions likely to produce great bodily harm or death, willfully causes or permits any elder or dependent adult to suffer, or inflicts thereon unjustifiable physical pain or mental suffering, or having the care or custody of any elder or dependent adult, willfully causes or permits the person or health of the elder or dependent adult to be injured, or willfully causes or permits the elder or dependent adult to be placed in a situation in which his or her person or health is endangered, is punishable by imprisonment in a county jail not exceeding one year, or by a fine not to exceed six thousand dollars ($6,000), or by both that fine and

imprisonment, or by imprisonment in the state prison for two, three, or four years.

You fought your eviction and won. Then, your landlord sued you for his court costs and the judge ruled in his favor leaving you with a $164,000 bill that you must pay or be subjected to eviction. We are three days away from your 100th birthday. Again, is this a birthday celebration or is it elder abuse?

A poem for Iris Canada

Tommi Avicolli Mecca

We should be coming
to listen to your stories
sitting on the floor
in a dimly lit room
perhaps in silken candlelight
memories floating all around us

instead we're with you
in a courtroom that wouldn't
know justice if it fell from the sky
we're out on the windy street
with our banners and slogans
trying desperately to be heard

you stand quietly watching
gripping your walker
100 year old eyes
that could never have imagined
that at your age you would
have to fight for your home

warrior
who doesn't have to
say a word
to inspire us

Eviction, elder abuse, and homelessness

Tiny Gray-Garcia
July 30, 2019, 48Hills.org

Why are so many elders and families on the street? They got evicted.

"I am being evicted from the home I was evicted to. I don't know where to go now. I want to come back to Oakland, but if I do I will end up homeless in Oakland."

Princess Beverly Williams, long-time Oakland resident, community organizer and elder, was holding back tears as she spoke to Po Peoples Revolutionary Radio last week.

Protesters remind us that evictions can be fatal.

Between February of 2014 to 2016, POOR Magazine made the case for elder and child abuse under penal codes 368 and 273a with over a dozen cases of elder and family evictions including 100 year old Black elder Iris Canada, Ron Likkers and Elaine Turner (who all died within days or weeks of being evicted from their longtime San Francisco homes) and presented them to District Attorney George Gascon who refused to file charges against the abusers. That continued a long-held practice of public officials protecting "private property ownership" over people.

Since then, the crisis we had has gotten so much worse. Because when elders and children are evicted it means abuse, trauma, homelessness, and often death for the victims.

RoofLESS radio unhoused reporters WeSearch report findings tells us that more than 88 percent of unhoused elders and families were evicted before they became unhoused.

In addition to the extreme rise in the silent killer of eviction, just in the last 5 years, there was a massive rise in the building of "market rate housing" with a cursory amount of so-called "affordable housing," which was never intended for us, the very low-income/no-income poverty skolaz as we call ourselves at POOR Magazine.

Ever since the RAD program caused the selling of public housing projects mortgages on the commodities market, launched by Obama cabinet member Julian Castro, we've seen an ongoing process of displacement for "renovation," reduction in units, and straight-up destruction of truly poor people housing all across the US. At the same time, there has been an extreme rise under State Sen. Scott Weiner of SB35-type bills, which give permits to what I affectionately call "devil-opers" aka corporate developers, to pursue the unbridled building of more and more new buildings (with little or no height restrictions) as long as they gave some tiny amount to affordable units.

This Housing Horror Story all resulted in the intentionally disconnected and un-linked homeless "counts" from San Francisco and Alameda county, which have been pouring in with numbers like 46 percent rise in Oakland alone, leaving people collectively shaking their heads.

Sadly, Princess Beverly was literally the 46th elder in a long line of elders, families with young children, and disabled adults who I have been speaking with those who are facing some kind of abuse, uninhabitable conditions in their low-income, Section 8 or market rate housing units, or straight up illegal/unlawful evictions just in the last two months.

"I was poisoned in one home due to a broken sewer pipe leaking into the basement only to move to another apartment filled with mold, my family ended up in the hospital behind all of this. We are so tired," said Vivi-T, formerly houseless, long-time POOR Magazine reporter, poverty skola, poet, and advocate. In Viv's case she was paying inflated, so-called "market rate" rents for each of these life-threatening homes which caused her minor children and her to end up in the hospital with breathing problems and ultimately homeless.

"After less than a year after evicting me they threw a coat of paint on the building and put it on the market for sale," said Aunti Frances. "This was after they said they were 'getting out of the rental property market' and giving their daughter a fresh start to own her own home."Auti Fances is a poverty skola with POOR magazine, co-founder of Homefulness and founder of the Self-Help Hunger Program. She was discussing her year-long battle to save her long-time home, only to lose it to the Ellis Act, which has caused the eviction of so many of the elders we and other advocates like housing Rights Committee and Causa Justa/Just Cause have fought for over the last several years.

"My family and I and this whole building almost burned to death and the landlords said I complain too much," said Sharena Diamond Thomas, a low-income mother of four, long-time Oakland resident and founder of Peoples Community Medics as she re-counted her horrible struggle to stay in her Section 8 housing even when the landlords refused to fix the habitability issues at the buildings peril. She received a notice to move, after Section 8 refused to approve the buildings housing voucher, even though her family underwent so much stress and trauma.

All of these aunties, mamas, and grandmamas have been made homeless or threatened with homelessness in the last year, due to the illegal or just plain unethical moves of what I call, scamlords (sometimes referred to as slumlords).

But the reality is for every elder or family we hear about who musters up the strength to fight back, there are literally hundreds we don't hear about who like my mama used to say walk softly on Mama Earth and just pick up and move into the card-board motels (homelessness)—families like me and my mama who before we became conscious would just take our hefty bags and sleep in our car or sleep outside if we had no car, even when there was no just cause to many of the evictions we survived.

This all resulted in me having to drop out of school in the 6th grade and permanently entering the underground economies that kept us alive. For our family, like so many others, eviction was trauma and violence and its rooted in the ongoing buying and selling of mama earth as a profit making strategy.

In capitalism (or krapitalism as I call it) this violent business known as "income property" too often involves rent raising, illegal evictions, and uninhabitable substandard housing, house-flipping, house selling and land hoarding – and it means thousands more people are homeless.

The insane and rising greed inherent in making more and more money off of the housing and unhousing of people is causing the insane rise in evictions, displacement and ultimately extreme gentrification and homelessness. This business model is no longer (if it ever was) a humane business.

It is why us youth and family poverty skolaz at POOR Magazine released the Hoarded Mama Earth report with a direct ask to un-sell Mama Earth so we could build/manifest more Homefulness projects (a homeless peoples self-determined movement to liberate mama earth and house homeless families happening right now in East Oakland with multi-nationed/First Nations guidance and permission and homeless peoples leadership.

But we are also seeking a pro-bono or civil rights law firm to help us re-file these criminal charges against these scam lords.

No matter how you try to wash it or dress it up, eviction is still elder and child abuse—which causes massive homelessness.

Beautiful to Broken Elevator to Bed Bugs: My 17 Years at Acton Courtyard Apartment Complex

Leroy F. Moore, Jr.
Media statement re: 1370 University Ave., Berkeley

Leroy F. Moore Jr., pictured here with POOR Magazine's Tiny Gray-Garcia, has lived in the Acton Courtyard Apartments in Berkeley for 17 years, experiencing the same difficulties disabled people report facing due to neglect of subsidized housing all over the country, from broken elevators to bedbugs. – Photo: San Francisco State University

It was 2004-2005 when I saw Acton Courtyard go up because I lived next door in a small studio. I saw an empty lot grow into a beautiful state of the art, large apartment complex. I was excited for a chance to go from a studio that was so small that I had to go outside to change my mind. I was new to Berkeley because, like many others, I was gentrified from the Mission District in San Francisco. I pulled all the strings to get an emergency housing voucher—getting letters from the Mayor of Berkeley and from Representative Barbra Lee, and other housing advocates. Plus an agency for people with disabilities helped out a lot! I was one of the first groups of people to move into Acton Courtyard and it was beautiful, clean, and came with cable, free WiFi, and more. The beauty didn't last as the property changed owners consistently. Original residents started to move out. That's when the

Equity Residential started to come after me, with notes and phone calls saying that I didn't pay rent for months. After going through the hassle of dealing with my bank to prove that they were wrong, I then realized another long-time resident was dealing with the same harassment. Then came the broken elevator in 2015 that lasted almost a month over the Thanksgiving holiday until we wrote an article in the Berkeley Planet and got a lawyer. That case took almost three years to settle. Our collective, sustained efforts strengthened local laws related to repairing elevators and the need for more inspections and notifications for residents when the work will be done.

Now, in 2021, my neighbors and I have seen a drastic cut back in the upkeep of the building—spots on the dirty carpet to dead plants to racist stickers to urine in the elevator. It has been a slow crawl to criminal malfeasance, which happens in buildings serving low- and no-income tenants by landlords who don't care. I found out that the new owner sold the other properties that were nicer compared to Acton Courtyard. Equity Residential tried to sell Acton Courtyard but no one wanted it. In 2016, I asked if I could transfer to another Berkeley unit before they sold them off. The landlord told me that it was an eight-year waiting list just to transfer to another building. At the same time, I would come home from college campus lectures from places from New York City to Toronto and see a three-day eviction notice. It happened over and over again! Another change was the so-called upper-class residents leaving quickly. Acton Courtyard became a building for only low-income residents and that's when the cut back of services in the building started with firing the live-in manager to keeping the carpet clean to letting plants die.

I know that the cut backs on the upkeep of the building have led to the year-long outbreak of bed bugs that infested my apartment in Fall 2020. And because the landlord has not taken this outbreak of bed bugs seriously, I had to stay in a local hotel for almost on my own dime and with help from friends. I started typing this from my second hotel stay in March 2021, because of an infestation of bed bugs. Both times, my community, aka Poor Magazine and friends,

In 2015, managers of Acton Courtyard Apartments in Berkeley became notorious for failing for weeks to fix broken elevators in the complex, which houses multiple disabled individuals and families who became trapped in their apartments, unable to leave as a result of the severe negligence of the building by property manager Equity Residential. – Photo: Equity Residential

saved me by helping me throw 95% of my clothes and furniture out and raise emergency funds to put me up in a hotel.

The first time I was away from my apartment for almost two months between a hotel and an offer from a friend to stay at her place. In turn, the landlord offered me $1500.00 to reimburse my hotel stay and the contract they wanted me to sign said that Acton Courtyard did the heat treatment to kill the bed bugs. In addition, I must bring up that before my friend and Poor Magazine got me into a hotel, the landlord was rude to me and my sister. They told me that it was up to me to clean the apartment and get it ready for the treatment. When I reminded them that I have certain accommodations as a disabled person they told me, "Maybe your family or in-home support person can help me clean"! Before I moved back into my place in January 2021, I called the city to come inspect my place. The city inspector came and saw two bed bugs. On January 16, 2021, I moved back in my place and noticed that the landlord hadn't cleaned the carpet so I hired a company to deep clean my carpets on my dime. Two weeks back in my apartment I noticed I was beginning again to itch then two bed bugs appeared on my white pillowcase. I stayed as long as I could handle it. Once again my friends came in and got me to the same hotel in March 2021. The city came out again and noticed bed bugs in their own traps that they pùt down in my apartment, plus two bed bugs on my bed. The company that my building hired to treat the bed bugs had this conversation with me:

Bedbug company guy: It's getting better.
Leroy: Look on my pillow.
Bedbug company guy: But it's only two and only in the living room.
Leroy: But as you see there is nothing in the bedroom and I sleep in the living room where the city person found three in their trap and as you can see on my pillow and sheet— at least three!
Bedbug company guy: But Leroy, you have to admit it's getting better!
Leroy: But, nevermind......

I started writing this on March 16th, 2021, my last night in the hotel. After not hearing from my landlord on when the treatment would be over and when it would be safe to move back in, I emailed to ask when the treatment would be done. They emailed me back to say that yes the treatment was done and it was safe to move back in. Throughout this bedbug situation my friends and the organization Poor Magazine have not only put me up at a hotel but have helped throw away 95% of my clothing and furniture and buy and wash new clothes. They also started a fundraiser and made sure I had food! As I make my way back to my apartment for the second time after being dis/misplaced, my confidence in my landlord to do the right thing, like treating the whole building or at least my neighbors, is on zero. So that's why the only option is to write my story and also look for another place to live in Berkeley!

Hold Up, Hotel Living?

BA going for a Ph.D.
Krip-Hop worldwide &
Obama wanted me
Hold up, hotel living?

Nightmare is the american dream
Forget Ghostbusters I'm calling The A Team
Never wanted white picket fence
Hold up I didn't ask for hotel living
Yeah Stevie Wonder, take me to Africa
Krip-Hop in liberal media
Still have to rely on Go Fund Me
Still not enough, hold up another day of hotel living
BA going for a Ph.D.
Krip-Hop worldwide &
Obama wanted me
Hold up, hotel living?
Poverty industry
Keeping us down and chasing
That pieces of paper, white & green
Wanted to put Harriet Tubman on it, caught us dreaming
Tubman let two off, pop pop
Going back to the roots of Hip-Hop
Where we can see the raw politics & politicians' politricks
Hold up, hotel living
No room service
two stars there is a difference
Between Beverly Hills Inn & Holiday Inn in the Hood
Next room from me is I.C.E. with their sets of eyes
Hold up can't go outside
COVID 19 & POLICE, is this my time
Going back home, rent free
No more hotel living
I was ready to go
He/She/They said "no it's not your turn!
I look over you so you can continue your work!"
But hold up wtf, more hotel living
"You got to believe
Do you feel me
Leroy, this is nothing

You can handle this!"

Leroy F. Moore Jr.
3/14/21

March 19, 2021: Hold up! I went on Berkeley Tenants Union to speak to a lawyer. It cost $5.00 to type questions and then they gave me an option to get a call from a lawyer for $60.00. So I took it and paid them. That was yesterday, still no call. WTF. You can't tell me that the city is not in the pocket of the landlord.

I emailed the landlord to let them know that more bed bugs appeared after I returned. Their reply: "Those bed bugs you saw may be coming out due to the pesticide treatment. If we still see them two weeks from now, then it will be a problem. That's why I would like to wait two weeks before setting the traps in your apartment unit." The first time I returned to my place my neighbors said I looked healthier and I did notice that dark circles around my eyes were slowly disappearing. The second time I returned to 1370 University Ave. and saw bed bugs on my pillow, I decided to sleep in the bathroom—sometimes in a chair and sometimes in the tub. After a few days, I noticed my feet and my lower legs started to swell up. A friend offered that my feet were swelling because I was sleeping in the chair. I had no choice but to return to my bed. To be clear—this was at the same time that my landlord and a city employee were telling me that I was overreacting and to just wait a couple of days and the bed bugs would be gone.

Sleeping in the Bathroom

I didn't want to write this song
It's just not right it so so wrong
My bed has bed bugs
Sleeping in the bathroom, I need a hug
The city says it's getting better
As bed bugs make a ladder
To get to my pillow
Eye to eye, as I kill it I have no sorrow
I'll be sleeping in the bathroom tomorrow

Scratching the etch over and over
The city says it's getting better
As they form a ladder trying to suck my blood
I didn't want to write this song
It's just not right it so so wrong
My bed has bed bugs
Sleeping in the bathroom, I need a hug
At night my bed they flood
Wake up in the morning and they are gone
I'm etching all day this is so wrong
Another night in the bathroom with a fat bong
Got to get high cause I can't believe this is my life
Every month I still pay my rent on time
Slumlord I want to take your life
As The Coup's song plays over and over
Have you tried sleeping in the bathtub
My skin I'm trying to rub
To smooth my bones as it hits fiberglass
Relief, finally, not scratching my ass
I didn't want to write this song
It's just not right it so so wrong
My bed has bed bugs
Sleeping in the bathroom, I need a hug
How did it end up like this
This is some bullshit
From the bedroom to the living room
Now sleeping in the bathroom

Leroy F. Moore Jr.
2:50 am 3/20/21

March 24, 2021: Knock! Knock! Yes it was my freakin' landlord just now wanting to spray! Yeah, no notice! No nothing! I told them to send me an email so I can put it in my freakin' calendar! WTF!

March 25, 2021: I just want to note that yesterday, March 24th, 2021, Acton Courtyard Apartments and the bedbug company knocked on my door to spray around my apartment. I told them to give me notice by email and to come back tomorrow. Today another knock on the door—it's the bedbug company guy to spray. I said ok and he did. However, I never got that email to reschedule. Now I need to open the windows and leave for some time so it can air out!

March 29, 2021: The reporter who visited Leroy's apartment on March 21, 2021 called me to let me know that he found four bed bugs in his place (not in Acton Courtyard) this morning. As of March 30, 2021, I have not seen more bed bugs in my apartment at this time.

I've lived at Acton Courtyard for just about 17 years—experiencing some good times, ongoing harassment from Equity Residential, and now bed bugs and throwing away 95% of my things and risking my health. The handwriting is on the wall saying that I must continue my search for a new place to live in Berkeley! Me and the Krip-Hop Nation that I founded have big plans and we want to continue our work in Berkeley, establishing a Krip-Hop Institute and becoming the Berkeley Poet Laureate one day. So as you can see, I must remain in Berkeley.

Poverty Tows to Palestine-The Violence of Settler Colonial Evictions Across Mama Earth

Lisa "Tiny" Gray-Garcia
May 24, 2021, *SF Bay View*

"If they tow my van I will die, I have nowhere else to go," reported POOR Magazine RoofLESS radio reporter Charles M, 68, lifelong San Francisco resident. Charless is houseless, landless, and disabled and lives in his van. San Francisco, like Oakland and so many other cities across the U.S., has increased its towing, "sweeping," "cleaning," and related removal projects of houseless peoples. This includes our sleeping bags, belongings, tents, vans, RVs, and cars throughout the pandemic. And as all of us who have struggled with homelessness know, once they take everything from us we run an increased risk of death by exposure, polLice terror, and illness.

"They are increasing the tows of houseless peoples RVs and vans," said Sam Lew, an organizer, advocate, and badass with End Poverty Tows Coalition who spoke with Po Peoples Radio last week.

From Frisco to Kashmir

"Where will I go?" asked Zooni Begam, 108 years old, as she squatted on the ground outside her house located in the village of Zilsidora,

108 year old Kashmiri elder Zooni Begam facing colonial eviction.

Jabbad, hidden in the vast jungle of central Kashmir's Budgam District. "I was born here. My parents also lived here. We have been living here for ages. How can the government make us homeless all of a sudden?"

Huma Dar, a fierce Kashmiri warrior for truth, introduced the story of Zooni to a panel entitled Degentrifying Academia sponsored by POOR Magazine, Indigenous Peoples Organizing for Change, Krip Hop Nation, and the Ethnic Studies Library at UC Berkeley in April. The goals of the panel, lovingly moderated by Dr. Fuifui Niumetolo, was launched by Leroy Moore and me before the pandemic to connect the land struggles of Indigenous, houseless Black, Brown, and Disabled peoples across Mama Earth. We strive to achieve collective land liberation from the colonial terror of evictions and removal that continue today.

Huma added that this is just the tip of the iceberg. It doesn't even mention the genocidal ethnic cleansing of 1947-1950 when up to a million Muslims (out of a total population of ~4 million at that time) were massacred or forcibly exiled out of the state by the Indian Army and the army of the draconian Hindu colonizing ruler, Hari Singh. Nor do they mention the more than ~6700 mass & unmarked graves unearthed in Kashmir, which India refuses to do DNA testing on to return people to their families.

Youth and families in the streets of San Francisco show solidarity with Palestine.

From Oakland to Palestine

"There is no way I'm leaving this neighborhood unless I'm dead," said a resident of Sheikh Jarrah, a Palestinian neighborhood in East Jerusalem, requesting anonymity for fear of retribution by Israeli authorities. "It's been 65 years that I've lived in this neighborhood," they concluded.

Across Mama Earth, the colonial terror of removal, eviction, sweeps, and gentrifUKation (as I call it) is a common thread. Rooted in the original genocide called colonization, which has terrorized Indigenous peoples across Mama Earth for centuries, continues today from West Papua to West Huchuin (Oakland). It is pushing people and lives out, killing elders, abusing and traumatizing children, and desecrating Indigenous ancestors to make way for "commerce," more houses, different people and/or the lie of "cleanliness" code for land without oppressed people. But the root of it all is that ownership of Mama Earth has always been a settler colonial lie and a bad one at that. Mama Earth is not infinite. You can't keep buying, selling destroying, and demolishing her forever.

Iris Canada, 100 year old Black Elder resident of San Francisco evicted from her home of over 40 years.

"I can't believe you are doing me like this Peter (Owens)," said Iris Canada, to the new "owner" of her home of over 40 years who evicted her. Iris was a 100 year old Black elder who died after recording that message, because as POOR Magazine and this poverty skola have said and barely survived, eviction is elder and child abuse. Iris was one of the few remaining Black residents of what us gentriFUKed peoples of San Francisco call the FilNoMore, aka Fillmore District. In the 70's, this area was decimated by the moves of Urban Renewal, re-named by all who were victims of it- Negro Removal, led by head gentriFUKer aka devil-oper (I like to re-name the colonial terms to express their true impact) Justin Herman, and continues to this day.

Since the well- documented "dot-com" boom of the 90's, working class, low-income, Black, Brown, poor white, disabled, and Indigenous residents of San Francisco and Oakland have suffered the ongoing terror and abuse of eviction. Countless fights led by organizers and advocates have ensued. Land trusts have sometimes been brokered, enabling the elders to stay housed. But by and large, it has resulted in the slow bleed of removal of working class and poor people from the Bay Area, which many times results in our permanent displacement and death.

Altar for Mario Gonzalez created/sponsored by the Oakland Brown Berets and Tele-Jaguar at a ceremony for him held at the location of his murder.

Luis Gongora Pat, an Indigenous Mayan father and worker, was evicted and then killed by poLice for being houseless in the gentriFUKED mission.

Ron Likkers, an Indigenous elder, was evicted and then died two weeks later.

Gerry Ambrose, a domestic laborer, died from the violence/ trauma and poverty caused by the eviction of her and her whole family from their home of 43 years in San Francisco.

Desiree Quintero, a houseless woman killed from the violence of sweeps in Santa Cruz.

Steven Taylor, a houseless resident of San Leandro, was murdered by poLice for having a mental health crisis in public.

Mario Gonzalez, who made the mistake of "tweeking" and possibly being houseless in Klanameda.

Once we are ancestors, we are also not seen and our sacred burial lands are continually desecrated as in the struggle for West Berkeley Shellmound. Or our bodies and relatives are viewed as something to study and profit off of or just warehouse, displaced and disposed of.

From Left: Corrina Gould, Leroy Moore, Tracey Bell Borden, Aunti Frances Moore and Tiny on the Stolen Land/Hoarded Resources Tour thru Akkkademia—photo by Brooke Anderson.

Anthro-Wrongology and Arkkkeology

"The ongoing occupation of our territories means that our ancestors, and in turn us their living descendants, have to continually resist erasure and being categorized as less than human. The disease of capitalism and private land ownership necessitates that we no longer exist in order for them to justify the destruction of our sacred sites, like the West Berkeley Shellmound and the hoarding of thousands of our ancestors at institutions like UC Berkeley," said land liberator, warrior, and prayer bringer of the Ohlone/Lisjan Nation and POOR Magazine Elephant Council leader and co-founder of Sogorea Te' Land Trust.

POOR Magazine launched our 2021 Stolen Land/Hoarded Resources Tours into Akkkademia on May 5th. We did this because Akkkademia (I re-named this more appropriately) plays a huge role in the perpetuation of land-stealing, resource hoarding, and ware-housing of Indigenous, Black, and Brown ancestors and culture. The warehousing of Ohlone/Lisjan ancestors at UC Berkeley and "storing" of the bones of children of the MOVE Africa Family by Princeton University and University of Pennsylvania are just two of the many reasons this poverty skola re-names these departments and perpetra-tors, Anthro-WrongOLOGY and Arkkkeaology.

"Entire blocks of communities in Philly were stolen by Temple University," said Galen Tyler, another powerful poverty skola and truth-teller with the Poor People's Economic Human Rights Campaign and #PoorPeoplesArmy out of Philadelphia. Galen presented at the DegentriFYing Academia panel, connecting the dots of gentriFU-Kation and land grabs for what I call the Dorm Industrial Complex, which is exactly what's threatening People's Park and 1921 Walnut Street in Berkeley.

From West Papua to West Huchuin (Oakland)

"While our demonstrations were entirely peaceful, the Indonesian police were determined to use brute force to crush them. Such mass arrests and brutality are becoming increasingly common in West Papua and it is estimated that in the last two months, nearly 3,000 West Papuan people have been arrested by the Indonesian authorities." There is gold to extract so the West Papuan Indigenous peoples are seen merely as an obstacle stopping this violent extraction from Mama Earth, whether it means the death of the Kashmiri Forest Dwellers, West Papuan Indigenous peoples, or West Oakland RV dwellers.

Benny Wanda, independence leader from West Papua.

West Oakland Sweeps of Houseless Peoples

"CalTrans is backing out on agreements made with residents & moving forward with evictions during the current pandemic …," shared EFAM (Essential Food and Medicine), a group that has helped to build a powerFUL clinic and other beautiful services within a houseless community in West Oakland, called Cob on Wood. This community has faced endless violent sweeps due to the fact that the poltricksters don't want to see houseless people. The nearby "land-Lord" (Fred Crave) and Killtrans (my name for that agency) want to profit off the land where houseless people have peacefully parked their RVs and cars for years.

All across the Bay and the United Snakes, these evictions, tows, and sweeps (equating humans with trash) have continued throughout a pandemic, causing people to die of exposure, not COVID.

It's controversial to connect these dots. A lot of organizers who can "feel" and organize and throw down for Indigenous people's global struggles have no interest in seeing the connections to houselessness, disabled elders struggling with sweeps, evictions, and gentriFUKations.

In addition, revolutionaries and even land liberators often call out for reparations and land-back for Black, Brown, and Indigenous peoples but cannot see the connections to houseless peoples or even the notion of Mama Earth itself not being a commodity.

Formerly houseless/landless, youth, adults, and elders from Homefulness.

I humbly propose in this story, as a formerly houseless daughter of a disabled, Indigenous trauma survivor, and later houseless mama of my Sun, and co-founder, visionary of Homefulness, a houseless, landless peoples solution to homelessness, to not only expand and connect the dots of settler terrorism to include landless poor peoples who are being swept, evicted, towed and destroyed every day in every colonial city across Amerikkka but to further that as land liberators working for true liberation, to please re-consider the narrative of land use itself. My argument is that the goal of revolutionaries should not be "ownership" at all.

#UnSellMamaEarth & #UnSettleMamaEarth.

No matter who does the "owning" of the colonial lies (I mean Laws) about MamaEarth's use, it is a set up from the get-up to evict, remove, and displace every poor and Indigenous person, over time. That as I have stated before, even the notion of "land trust" is rooted in a removal platform. Land trusts come with an expiration date, embedded with the eventual profiting off of. This is why we houseless, Indigenous, disabled peoples at Homefulness are working really hard to spiritually and legally UnSell Mama Earth and my newest goal and associated "hashtag" is to UnSettleMamaEarth—so please help us get that into the Hashtag lexicon.

The messiness of our connectedness is our liberation. Us houseless peoples from all four corners of Mama Earth have so much in common with houseless, landless First Nations Turtle Islanders, West Papuans, Kashmiris, Palestinians, and beyond. We really need to co-organize these fights against the Extraction terror of what CorpRape and poli-tricksters have been doing for 528 years and before to all of us. Not some of us.

Writing Visions of Homefulness

Otro Mundo Es Posible y Se Está Construyendo / Another World is Possible and is Already Being Built

Muteado Silencio

Like thousands of people, I have worked, cultivated, and planted seeds. Never to see or enjoy the fruits of my labor.

We have made and cleaned the most beautiful gardens that I have seen in my life in the mountains of Berkeley for people with money. Earning $10 an hour, we have built and managed houses with immense beauty. Only to never see them again.

We have silently obeyed the orders of the stewards, managers, and company owners; the owners of the houses, the owners of our checks, the owners of our lives. We have been forced into "obeying always in silence," but it does not always have to be this way.

In January 1994, a group called the Zapatistas (EZLN: the Zapatista National Liberation Army) emerged from silence. They came forth from the silence that used politicians and butlers, and carried the cries of injustice against Indigenous people and workers.

The Zapatistas began using a language that speaks of justice, land and freedom, always talking and working with each other. They do not use Twitter or Facebook, newspapers, or television. They do it face to face, people to people, village to village.

In the early hours of December 21, 2012, the EZLN came out of the shadow of injustice and corruption that still lives and breathes in Mexico today. It was rumored that they left five caracoles (villages). In total, there were over 40,000 Zapatistas in the streets of Chiapas.

The Zapatistas left a Press release:

http://enlacezapatista.ezln.org.mx/2012/12/30/el-ezln-anuncia-sus-pasos-siguientes-comunicado-del-30-de-diciembre-del-2012/

The press release of the Zapatistas said that little by little they are creating a world that we romanticize here in the United Snakes of Amerikkka. The Zapatistas have stopped believing in the lies of all politicians, political parties, and non-profit organizations that only bring misery and injustice.

"The land belongs to those who work the land" is not only a saying in Chiapas; it is an action in Zapatista communities.

Other communities have taken steps similar to those of the Zapatistas. In Cheran, Michoacan, the P'urepecha people took up arms after the Mexican government could not ensure the safety of the people. Here, organized crime has plundered the forests the people of the region depend on for survival.

> "Another world is possible, and is being constructed."

In Oakland, California, people are taking a stand too. In 29 years of life, I've always had to respond and obey my teachers, my employer, the people who sign my checks, the bad governments, the nonprofit organizations, and other authorities. But in June 2011, a group of workers, dreamers, displaced poor folks, migrants, mothers, uncles, aunts, grandmothers, and grandparents of different social classes took up a piece of land in East Oakland called Homefulness. The land originally belonged to the Ohlone people, the Natives of this Land, and so with permission and humility the dream of Homefulness became a reality.

With the help and support of the community we tore up the concrete and released Tonanzin, Mother Earth, to plant seeds of hope and resistance. We created a garden of herbs and vegetables called Pachamama Garden in East Oakland. The Pachamama garden was a real community effort. With the help of groups like Take Back the Land, ROOTS, Decolonize Oakland, and Phat Beets and through the efforts of volunteers and community members, we planted carrots, cilantro, lettuce, oregano, and other herbs. We did it all without the help of foundations, non-profits, or pimps. The project was completed only with the help of the community and a grassroots organization called POOR Magazine, Prensa Pobre.

POOR Magazine is creating, developing, and spreading hope and strength for the community of Homefulness. In these times when it is difficult to get a plate of food, Homefulness offers and shares

food with our community, including fruits and vegetables from the Pachamama Garden.

In the not too distant future, POOR Magazine plans to build a housing center, media center, and cultural center for our community at Homefulness following our principles as a very grassroots organization, without asking the poverty pimps, foundations, or non-profit for their crumbs.

New Resident Stories

Westyn: I guess my story has to start with my parents, without whom there would be no me! My parents were traumatized and colonized humans, with their own distant hopes and dreams, long before I ever called them by the sames "Mom" and "Dad". My mom crossed the false U.S border at a young age with her family from Nicaragua and was ridiculed her entire life for her brown skin and her native Spanish, in addition to a tumultuous home life/family dynamic. My dad came from a mixed Japanese/Arab home and endured severe emotional abuse from his colonizer father who eventually left the family to fend for themselves. My parents did their best for me though and I was raised in Alameda. Ironic that my whole life, we lived paycheck to paycheck, with one of my biggest fears being people would realize my dad and I had "nothing" and shared a one-bedroom apartment that I never brought anyone home to.

I honestly don't even know where to begin with how I got here other than that this is one of the only places i've ever been where I feel free and encouraged to be my real, whole self, traumas included and for that reason, I want to see Homefulness flourish as far and wide as possible to spread the healing.

J.V: Homefulness, a landless movement built from love and peace, a community rising in the heart of the imperialist beast. Shouts of liberation we want to be free! Pig terror is real for you and me. Building the future leaders in an unjust environment. Lets do this together because we know for revolutionaries there is no retirement. ... As you first walk into Homefulness, and see this collective of people that is an example of beautifulness.

Israel: Like all people in struggle I deal with trauma and recovery—I have struggled with addictions, poverty and homelessness. Homefulness is giving me a chance to breathe and heal and we realize that together we as poor people can build our own solutions.

Emeterio: A mi me gustaría vivir en una casa o en un cuarto porque yo vivo en una ven aproximadamente 7 años y para mi es una muy buena oportunidad de vivir en una casa y también poder tener el privilegio de vivir como cualquier ciudadano.

I'd like to live in a house or in a room because I live in a van approximately 7 years and for me it is a very good opportunity to live in a house and also be able to have the privilege to live like any citizen.

Ingrid: ¿Por qué quiero vivir aquí? Porque parezco pelota rodando de un lado a otro me vine de Guatemala pues estuve pasando por un problema muy grande con el que fui mi esposo me golpeada llegue a casa de mi mama y mi hermana me hacía la vida imposible decía mentiras para que me golpearan allí mis dos hermanos menores llegué a Estados Unidos. Mi hermano me golpeó. Llegué donde mi hermana y mi cuñada abusaron de mi y los problemas crecieron no aborte por temor de dios pero tenía miedo de no amar a mi hijo.

Ellos me golpeaban los dos y luego me quede en la calle con mi hijo, luego me fui donde una amigo y ella me ayudó a encontrar un lugar luego el hombre me maltrataba y nos serraba la puerta. No podíamos usar el baño luego teníamos que hacernos en un bote o en la calle nuestras necesidades después me fui a la 24 y potrero allí estábamos me o mi hijo y yo perro la señora me humillaba después llego a mi hijo y él empezó a fregarnos luego nos fuimos a South San Francisco y todo parecia bien pero luego empezaron los problemas con los vecinos pero por lo menos nosotros estábamos bien pero mi hija se fue y yo no puedo pagar tanta renta.

Why do I want to live here? Because I seem like a ball rolling from one side to the other I came from Guatemala well I was experiencing a really big problem with who I went my husband hit me I arrived at the home of my mom and my sister made my life impossible told lies so that they would hit me there my two younger siblings I arrived to the United States. My brother hit me. I arrived at where my sister and my sister in law abused me and the problems grew I did not abort out of fear of god but I was afraid of not loving my son.

They hit me both of them and then I stayed in the street with my son, then I went to a friend's and she helped me to find a place then the man mistreated me and closed the door on us. We could not use the bathroom then we had to do our necessities in a tin or in the street after I went to the 24 and potrero there I was or my son and I were but the lady humiliated me later my son arrived and he began to wash us then we went to South San Francisco and all seemed well but then problems started with the neighbors but at least we were okay but my daughter left and I cannot pay so much rent.

Alex: Razones por las cuales quiero vivir aqui #1 porque donde vivo ay señoras blancas como papel que son unas racistas como si ellas fueran las nativas de America, porque la cuesta mucho trabajo a mi mama para pagar la renta y llega muy cansada del trabajo y ya no tiene energía para hacer más

#2 para que nuestra familia (mis tías hipócritas) ya no nos molesten y podemos vivir en paz

#3 para estar rodeando de gente que sí soporta y levanta el espíritu y no lo destroza

> *Reasons why I want to live here #1 because where I live there are ladies white like paper that are racists like if they were the natives of America, because it costs my mom a lot of work to pay the rent and she arrives very tired from work and no longer has energy to do more*
>
> *#2 so that our family (my hypocrite aunts) no longer bother us and we can live in peace*
>
> *#3 to be surrounded by people that do support and uplift the spirit and do not destroy it*

Indigenous Mamaz Herstories on Poverty in a Pandemic

Teresa: Mi nombre es Teresa. Soy Mama de 5 hermosos hijos, 4 hombres y una hermosa hija. 5 hermosos nietos, 3 hermosas nietas y 2 hermosos nietos. Soy de la ciudad de Mazatlán Sinaloa, Larazos. Yo emigre a este país por la maldita pobreza porque yo quería un mejor futuro para mis hijos. Ha sido difícil vivir en este país pero he luchado mucho para sacar adelante. Yo recuerdo el ultimo dia en mi

tierra fue muy triste despedirme de lo que más amaba mis hijos, mi tierra, mi familia. Mis lágrimas no dejaban de salir de mis ojos pero la emoción de soñar en el futuro de mis hijos me hace volver realidad y llegar hasta donde quieren llegar.

> *My name is Teresa. I am a mother of 5 beautiful children, 4 men and a beautiful daughter. 5 beautiful grandchildren, 3 beautiful granddaughters, and 2 beautiful grandsons. I am from the city of Mazatlán Sinaloa, Larazos. I emigrated to this country because of damn poverty, because I wanted a better future for my children. It has been difficult living in this country. I have struggled a lot to get ahead. I remember the last day in my land. It was very sad to say goodbye to what I loved the most, my children, my land, my family. My tears kept coming out of my eyes, but the emotion of dreaming about my children's future makes me come back to reality and get to where I want to go.*

Carmen: Mi nombre es Carmen Rodarte. Soy de un rancho de Zacatecas, México. Yo me vine de mi lugar de nacimiento porque allá mi mamá no tenía muchos recursos para darnos de comer. Deje 2 hijos con ella, cuando me vine a Estados Unidos, cuando llegue tenia 17 años empecé a trabajar y mandarle dinero a mi mama para mis hijos.

Después de años me junte, tuve a mi hija y de haber pasado. No tener donde vivir nos separamos después me fui a Salinas y allí encontré otra persona y tuve 3 hijos con él, pero después él hizo algo a mi familia demasiado fuerte. Él está ahora en la cárcel pero nos dejó muy dañada a mi y a mis hijos.

Ahora encontré a otro hombre pero creo que ha sido peor. Pues él solo quiso y quiere una relación a escondidas. Tengo 2 de él pero pues él tampoco me ayuda ni económicamente ni mucho emocionalmente.

Yo hago comida para vender y también cuponeo jabón shampoo para poder sacar. Para mis gastos y aun asi no puedo salir adelante y cubrir todos mis gastos. Pero con ellos de Prensa Pobre me he ayudado mucho con pañales y comida cada semana para mi y mi familia ya que somos muchos.

My name is Carmen Rodarte. I am from a ranch in Zacatecas, Mexico. I came to the United States from my place of birth because there my mother did not have many resources to feed us. I left 2 children with her when I came here. When I arrived, I was 17 years old. I started working and sending money to my mother for my children.

After years I got together with a man. I had my daughter and it happened. Not having a place to live, we separated later and I went to Salinas. There I found another person and I had 3 children with him, but then he did something very heavy to my family. He is now in jail, but he left me and my children very damaged.

Then I found another man, but I think it was worse. Well, he just wanted and continues to want a secret relationship. I have 2 (kids) from him but he doesn't help me financially or emotionally.

I make food to sell and I also supply shampoo soap to be able to take care of my expenses. Even then, I cannot get ahead and cover all my expenses. But with Poor Magazine I have been helped a lot with diapers and food every week for me and my family since there are many of us.

Edith: Mi nombre es Edith Herrera. Yo vengo de México, la diferencia entre Mexico y aqui, Estados Unidos es la clase de vida pues cuando uno está allá, piensa que todo será fácil pero no al llegar aquí. Es muy difícil pues uno se encuentra con muchas dificultades todo es trabajar para poder sostenerse pagar vivienda, biles, pero sin duda alguna el estar aquí en este país es mejor por que hay mucho mas recursos de ayuda. Es muy importante saber cómo respetar las reglas de este país. Hay muchas ayudas para nosotros la gente que lo necesita.

Mi país tiene mucha violencia. No es vida para los niños. Me gustaría que mi país fuera como Estados Unidos. Yo vine aquí por una mejor vida y para que mis hijos tengan mejor oportunidad.

My name is Edith Herrera. I come from Mexico. The difference between Mexico and the United States is the kind of life. When you are there (Mexico), you think that everything will be easy but not when you get here. It is very difficult because one encounters many difficulties. Everything is about working to be able to support paying for housing and bills. But without a doubt, being here in this country is better because there are much more resources for help. It is very important to know how to respect the rules of this country. There are many people who need it.

My country has a lot of violence. It is not a life for children. I would like my country to be like the United States. I came here for a better life and for my children to have a better opportunity.

Liliana: I was born in a hot land with temperatures over 100 degrees, where you can even cook eggs on the pavement. It is a desert where poor people make their little houses wherever they can find them—cardboard houses, clay sheets, iron, fabrics, mattress wires.

I remember waking up in the morning to the smell of my grandmother's flour tortillas. Some tortillas were the size of a pizza. It is where I cooked in a horinela.

I remember my grandmother's humble little house, where I spent my first 6 years. It only had two little rooms made out of materials. But it had a large courtyard where my imagination was a mechanical

businesswoman, a pilot. Where there is factory work there is work but a lot of poverty.

At the age of 6, I emigrated to the United States. The first place I came to was San Francisco in the Tenderloin, where I found many challenges as a new place. Wherever you look, from being so young at 6 years one shouldn't see many homeless people. Sleeping on the street had an impact on me. I thought that in the United States there were no homeless. For being the richest country, it has no solutions for poor people.

Yo nací en tierra caliente más 100 grados. Donde puedes cocinar hasta huevos en el pavimento. Es un desierto donde la gente pobre pudo hacer sus casitas donde puedes encontrar. Casas de cartón, láminas barro, fierro, cartera, telas, alambres de colchón.

Recuerdo levantándome en la mañana con el olor de tortillas de harina de mi abuela. Unas tortillas del tamaño de una pizza. Donde cocine en una horinela.

Recuerdo la casita humilde de mi abuela. Donde pasé mis primeros 6 años. Solamente tenía dos cuartitos de material.

Pero un grande patio donde mi imaginación fue una empresaria mecánica., una pilota. Donde hay trabajo de fábrica hay trabajo pero muchísima pobreza.

A los 6 años emigre a los Estados Unidos. El primer lugar que llegue fue a San Francisco en Tenderloin, donde me encontré muchos retos como un lugar nuevo. Donde mire chucho que a los 6 años no debería ver mucha gente desamparada. Durmiendo en la calle eso fue un impacto para mi, yo pensé que en Estados Unidos no había desamparados. Por ser el país más rico no tiene soluciones para la gente pobre.

What About Me? The Homeless Youth in Amerikkka

Queennandi Xsheba PNN KEXU

Avan was a teenager with a kind soul who was alone and houseless. He lived in a tent in San Francisco and struggled greatly trying to navigate the winding road called life. According to his close friends, he barely had any family support or guidance so he had to learn how to take care of himself. This was a difficult task because after all, he was just a kid. It was said that earlier this month he was near his tent and allegedly fell off a cliff, suffered a severe head injury, and drowned in the freezing bay water. Avan's friends were having a hard time accepting the alleged "freak accident" calling the fall "suspicious" and "not taken seriously."

A candlelight vigil was held for the teen by the water and many of his peers and family members attended to honor Avan. Although there were mixed feelings about how he was casted out and forced to fend for himself, his friends remained respectful to the elders and other folks who had allegedly forgotten about him.

Unfortunately, It is difficult to obtain stability in an unstable nation and it doesn't matter if you are a man, woman, child, or elder. What is the real slap in the face is that the "powers that be" deliberately cut budgets and the need for push basic human rights to the back burner with a blazing flame. Many people have lost their jobs, homes, dignity,

and even their lives relying on a "Sssystem" that has shown us time and time again that we are nothing but "expendable assets"

But what happens to the kids that have no one to support them? What about the youth who have been shuffled around from foster home to foster home only to be given the boot at the age of 18 under the "maxed out, ass out" protocol? Many of these youngsters wind up in the streets engaging in any activity that encourages self-medication and self-criminalization thus further desensitizing any part of their being that is human. Then, they are blamed by those who have contributed in one way or another to the hell we are all catching.

It is the hell of seeing young folks give up on life completely after trying to hold down a job while living in a car because the rent is unaffordable, only to end up dying in a doorway from a drug overdose. Like the young female who is easily misguided by a "wolf in sheep's clothing" because she never had anyone in her whole life teach her about her worthiness so she bends to the will of those who exploit her just to have a meal and a roof over her head.

The scenarios mentioned above are all too common nowadays with not only the youth but with full grown adults as well. When you throw in the pandemic and the hopes of politicians passing a vote that won't allow the people to starve to death, that is enough nail-biting stress within itself.

Insead of it being against the law for folks to be poor and house-less, it should be illegal to have legislation put in place that allows for children to become houseless in the first place, and in some states removed from their families because of poverty. It also should be illegal to incarcerate kids just because their elders want to come to a "great country" to make a so-called "better life" for the generations that are to come. After all, Angelina Jolie cannot adopt all of the children.

"I'm starting to think that the rich in the world is safe, while the po' babies resting in a early grave." —Tupac Shakur

Homefulness & DeeColonize Academy

Corrina Gould

Link: youtu.be/1hRLuXN2Apk

… a house inside those spaces that you're living. So you've got the little people in the front room in the front house. And you've got the older kids in the back house. And you've got computers all set up for the older kids. You've got teachers from the community coming in and teaching them and you're pulling money out of the air to do that. And you've got folks that are coming in and bringing food. Everyday these kids have food. And somehow you figure out how to get gas to pay for these community vans that pick kids up and then take them home. Sometimes they don't have a home to go to and they spend the night. Right there at Homefulness.

This is Homefulness. This is what we're talking about. This is the community. This is how it's built. So, we talk about all of these stories that come into it. That's how we got to there. But this is still being built.

So then you put in the infrastructure. Who tells people that when you decide you want to build this dream that you have to spend $60,000 on pipes and wires, underneath the ground that you can't even see? How do poor people know that that shit happens? And then, to get told by the people, "Oh, our mistake. Downtown, the gas pipe actually isn't there, it's over here. So you have to give us some more money, even though it was our mistake." How do we know these kinds of things?

And then, our brothers and sisters that come here across these false borders that know how to do this work, we can't hire them because they don't have the papers that contractors have to have. And so we're sitting there paying these folks that are able to have that. And going through this money that we've been accumulating in this way that we can't figure out. Right? So this is what Homefulness is—is trying to figure out, how do we do that? How do we put solar panels up? How do we live off the grid? How do we do this? Then, not only that, but then we create these schools that go around and show people. This is how it's going to be done. Not just for us, but for everybody else. That this is a possibility, that folks can live this way.

And the reason I know that this is a possibility is because I know that in 2011, six years ago, almost to the day, we re-took a sacred place in my territory for 109 days. Right before Occupy, right before Standing Rock. Hundreds of people came together on the last 15 acres of open land, on the Karkin Straight, that was sacred to my ancestors. And the city of Vallejo was going to build a park on top of it. It was going to destroy two of our burial sites. It was the last standing ground of my ancestors before the missions came and took them away in 1810.

And we stood there with people from all over the world that paid for this stuff, just like at Standing Rock. They made sure there were tents there and that there was a fire going and that there was food for people. And nobody ever had to want anything. And people from all different walks of life came and had ceremony there. People came and they prayed and they stayed there. And we were under surveillance by all kinds of folks.

But we were able to stay there, and what we thought we were saving actually saved us. That land saved us. It gave us back our humanity. And we decided what needed to happen was that, with the 109 days that opened up our hearts and changed our lives forever, that we needed to redo that for people. Because just like in New York, where everything is built upon, everything that my ancestors once had is almost completely covered in cement and buildings. How do we bring the humanity back to living with each other again?

So, the Sogorea Te' Land Trust is the first urban Indigenous women's land trust in the country. Now there's land trusts all over, right? And mostly what people do is they put up these walls and they put up these chain link fences. It says, "Do not trespass." Right? For land trusts, because we're protecting it. For what? We're protecting it away from ourselves. We're protecting it away from being humans again. Because we know if we give ourselves a chance, if you've ever gone camping, if you've ever stayed away from your phone or electronics for more than seven hours—you know that you become in tune with yourself again. Something just feels better. Something just feels better.

And so that's what this is. Sogorea Te' Land Trust isn't about buying a huge piece of land, but repurchasing little blocks of land all over our

territory, so that we can talk about our history as Ohlone people. So that we can rebury our ancestors that were taken out of land, stolen from their own burial places. So that we can create these places where my grandchildren can learn their songs and dances again so that we can re-heal the land. So that's what Sogorea Te' Land Trust is about. It's about reminding ourselves of all these things.

I live in one of the most poverty stricken places in the Bay Area. I have a Habitat for Humanity house that I was actually able to help build with my kids. Right? So, I was blessed to do that. But so many people in that same neighborhood, that was there for many generations, there's no place for kids to play. There's no places where they can have a garden. There's no places where there's soil that they can play in. We know now, scientifically, that it's good for kids to play in dirt, that they need those microbes and all of that stuff in order to build healthy immune systems. We know all of that kind of stuff.

We also know, as human beings, that we actually need to be in the ground because it helps us to center ourselves. People are always talking about that. There's this book called Braiding Sweetgrass, if you guys have ever read it. It's a beautiful book by a Potawatomi woman. She's a biologist and she's learning about her language. And she said, there's a language of animacy in Potawatomi, that says you can be a bed, you can be a hill, to be something. We, in the English language, are all about nouns and not about verbs. She also talks about how every time she takes her students out and puts them into the ground to start working the ground, no matter where they come from in the world, after eight minutes they start to sing. That it's a natural process for human beings because we are supposed to do these things. We're supposed to have this natural connection. We're supposed to know where our food comes from. We're supposed to be a part of that.

And so, like Homefulness, the Sogorea Te' Land Trust is about reconnecting and creating this interdependence again. This way of living. And like Laure said, this whole thing out here that's happening is not going to last very long. And eventually we all have to figure out, how do we become humans again? How do we begin to not shut the door on our next door neighbors? How do we begin to even know what our next door neighbors' names are again?

Homefulness (from *Poverty Scholarship*)

Tiny Gray-Garcia

> *"From Removal to Reparations...From Houselessness to*
> *HOMEFULNESS...*
> *From indigenous lands stolen to budget crumbs throw-en—*
> *From affordable housing in name only to rights to a roof by*
> *any means necessary...*
> *From the cult of independence to the Revolution of*
> *inter-dependence...*
> *From poverty-pimped housing po-lice to*
> *Revolutionary equity for all Realized...!!!!"*

After 500 years of removal, GentriFUKation, Anthro-Wrong-ology, akkkademik studies, and philanthro-pimped capitalist compromises, and consumerist destruction POOR Magazine's family of landless, indigenous elders, ancestors, mamas, aunties, uncles, fathers and abuelitos, daughters and sons will be realizing the revolution that is Homefulness.

I pulled each torn lace a little more tightly through their broken shoelace holes. Leo brushed back his dread-locks with one hard push of his muscled hand. Muteado tightened the hair-tie that held his thick black braid in place. We were ready.

We had spent the last several weeks, months, years, and centuries preparing.

Our steps quicken, our breath gets heavier. The ancestors are with us now holding 520 years of genocide. Downtown Oakland was quiet, there was a stillness in the corporate nature landscape of Oscar Grant Plaza. Even the pigeons knew.

We, the evicted, incarcerated, bums, hobos, trash, domestic workers, day laborers/trabajadores, street husslaz, medicine people, mamaz, youth of color, elders, disabled, criminalized, profiled and crazy were walking into a battle to liberate stolen indigenous Ohlone land By Any Means Necessary.

We slowly climbed the marble steps of the colonizer's mansion, passing countless blood-stained file cabinets, computers, and locked rooms holding our stolen stories and the micro-fiche memories of genocidal treaties and the coordinated lines running across our poor bodies of color, our indigenous souls, our ancestors' spirits.

When we arrived there were no guns, or shouts or screams or machetes, only a soft weapon held to our throats, masked as a hand-shake, a smiling introduction hovering over a shiny conference tables.

Our weapon was heavy in our hands. The corners sharp and crisp. We shifted our feet to not drop them.

We had a 2pm appointment with our local councilperson.

The violence of a landless peoples' land liberation movement waged within a wite-supremacist system created with kolonizer HIS-Stories and values, rules, and laws based in clock-time, paper-theft, corporate law, and above all blood-stained Amerikkklan dollars is a different kind of revolution.

In the tradition of MOVE 9 meets the Zapatistas, the indigenous/poverty, migrante, disability, elder, youth, and mama skolaz at POOR Magazine/Prensa POBRE have been working steadfastly for the last 520 (indigenous peoples genocide), 220 years (chattel slavery's meta-phorical end in Amerikkka), and 16 years (the life of POOR Magazine) to manifest a landless peoples land liberation movement in the over-priced, gentrified streets of the Bay Area.

Like our hermano@s in Chiapas we are indigenous peoples in struggle but with an added oppression, we are urban, landless, indig-enous peoples in diaspora, removed, displaced, separated, stolen, immigrated, from our tribal lands of origin, with no hope of re-couping them in struggle to stay alive and work in humility with our Ohlone brothers and sisters who are the 1st nations people of this stolen land.

Like our sheroes and heroes in MOVE 9 we are located in a majority African descendent intentionally blighted and gentriFUKed neigh-borhood, but unlike them we are attempting to work within the city constraints of land use and real estate snakkkeing and politricksterism.

And like the Shackdwellers Union we are poor, we are landless, we are Po'Lice harassed, and we are always under attack by Po'Lice, politricksters, and land-LORD hustlers.

From the beginning we have been guided by our landless, poor, indigenous, multi-tribal elders and ancestors, our many spiritual guides, Orixas, Mama Earth's whispers, and Creators prayers.

Similar to our sheroes and heroes from the Black Panthers, we follow the Black Commune and most importantly we believe that The Revolution Will Not Be Melted in a Pot. We diligently work to honor the multiple languages, traditions, spirits, religions, and practices, both pre-and post-colonial of our many different family members, of our ancestral memories, of ourselves.

We work in solidarity with young people with race, class, and/or educational privilege. These young people humbly understand that their role is not to save us or lead us, but only to stand with us— and support visions for us and by us as they activate clear-headed reparations of wealth and access they have easy but unjust access to. They learn this through a constant process of learning and teaching and guiding by us as poverty skolaz.

The Homefulness project like the POOR Magazine revolution began with an indigenous, houseless mother and daughter. Our revolution began in the back seat of a car. Our revolution began with a poem, as we walk humbly through so much pain and with a story, and continue to operate always in a story.

One of the things that corporate-simulated non-profits demand is the separation of self and state. This is to ensure that when the philanthro-pimps tire of your work, they can handily drop you on your baby-heads and it isn't exactly genocide, because its only the death of an "organization," not a people, not a spirit, a dream, or a hope for a neighborhood.

So as poor people-led, indigenous people-led organizations we are very clear that our issues, our struggles, our resistance, and our healing are entwined with us as people-always.

How Not to Call the Popo

Frances Moore

Growing up in the sixties during the civil rights movement, there is a typical saying that a Black mother would tell her son, "Son, don't be walkin' with your hands in your pockets. The police will stop you and think you got a gun." I grew up with this fear of the police and that certainty of police terror runs through my veins today as an adult.

When I got raped by my roommate and a friend, I said to myself, "HELL NO, I'm not calling the police." I used another method of public humiliation. As we shared friends in common, I told all our friends and it was a constant reminder of his action. The humiliation was so great that he relocated. For one thing, living in the hood, to call the police, you would be considered a snitch. This was radical restorative justice without calling the police.

In the Black Panther Party, working at the Oakland Community School, when a child broke rules of conduct or offended another student, the child who committed the offense would be brought before a council of his peers. That council of students would then be the judges regarding the issue. The offensive issue would be discussed and an agreement of action would be finalized among the council of students.

Today, we at POOR Magazine/Homefulness practice the same principles. I sit on the Elephant Council as an elder where we discuss and make decisions as a group. We then decide on various topics and situations. Some are easy and some are very difficult. Oftentimes these difficult situations need more time. We would continue until we reached common ground.

We must learn in our community of people and develop our council. We must learn to handle our own affairs. In doing this we empower ourselves. We solve our own problems and provide our own solutions. Ultimately, we avoid the capitalist financial gain of the courts and police. We avoid the financial rip off that ends up destroying us.

Reprinted from *How to Not Call the Po'Lice Ever*, also available from poorpress.net

Unpaving the Way for a Decolonized Day—Asphalt-Lifting Day at HOMEFULNESS 2

Tiny Gray-Garcia

As some of you already know, the last 6 months, starting when we planned to break ground for a community garden in this poor peoples of color neighborhood under seize from deep real estate speculation, we have been grappling with real estate snakkkes and paper trail thieves tryin to get in the way of the landless peoples revolution that is HOMEFULNESS which after 15 years of struggle, gentriFUKation and resistance we were blessed to acquire some land to eventually build the inter-generational school, community garden and sweat-equity housing project for houseless families.

On Inter-dependence Day (July 5th) 2011—This land was blessed by poverty, indigenous, elder, disabilty and migrante skolaz as well as Corrina Gould, Jose Cuellar and Xochi Maez Valdez and a group of pro-bono architects are creating blueprints and a scale model for the project as we e-speak.

That said, we are now going foreward "By any means necessary" with the garden to bring healthy food to this (food desert) poor peoples of color neighborhood which will be what we do there until we can raise enough blood-stained amerikkkan dollaz to build the housing and school.

That said, we are planning to throw an asphalt lifting-garden preparing party on Sunday, Feb 26th starting @ 11:00 am. We need ALL the hands and help we can get. We are going to have to get debris boxes and jack-hammers, etc. We will be starting the day out with a prayer. children are welcome- and there will be an adult supervising—Bring food if u can- but Auntie Teresa, and Utopia will be bringing hot dogs, and hot links. We will also be filming—so all other media is also welcome.

PLEASE LET US KNOW IF U CAN HELP in any way- by emailing deeandtiny@poormagazine.org before the event!

Chapter 4

Bloodstained into Lovestained Bucks

ComeUnity Reparations &
Radical Redistribution to
MamaFest Homefulness

PeopleSkool

APPLY HERE

HTTP://WWW.RACEPOVERTYMEDIAJUSTICE.ORG/

PEOPLE SKOOL
OFFERED TWICE A YEAR
IN JANUARY & AUGUST

A DegentriFUKation/Decolonization Seminar by POOR Magazine/Prensa POBRE

IN-PERSON (OAKLAND) AND ON ZOOM!

Day 1 of the workshop is for poverty skolaz AND people with race, class and/or formal education privilege. It will center Poverty Scholarship & the medicine of poor, houseless and indigenous people-led movements & media.

Day 2 is for people with race, class and/or formal education privilege, aimed at service providers, media creators, educators, organizers, researchers, artists, legislators, policy-makers, donors/philanthropists, students, community members- anyone who wants to learn about following Black, Indigenous POC and poor leadership and aligning your work with poor people-led self determination movements.

When it comes to who's a poverty skola /a person with privilege, there's lots of "gray areas" in krapitalism -- email poormag@gmail.com if you need help figuring out where you land

Bank of CommUnity Reparations

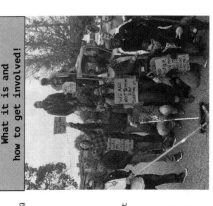

THE BANK OF COMMUNITY REPARATIONS

What it is and how to get involved!

COMMUNITY REPARATIONS FUNDS

Po' Mamaz Reparations Fund: Dedicated to redistributing resources directly to poor, unhoused and formerly unhoused single mamaz, (fathers) and children who are unable to afford rent, a drivable vehicle, diapers, food, and other emergency needs related to their survival and thrival.

Tech Reparations Fund: Dedicated to building/preserving the equity of poor and working class communities who have been displaced or are at risk of displacement due to the presence of Tech industries and their employees.

Homefulness Community Reparations Fund: Dedicated to building, launching and growing homefulness comm-UNITIES across Mama Earth. Homefulness is a self-determined landless people's solution to the housing crisis, and POOR Magazine is currently in the process of constructing a multi-unit housing complex in East Oakland to provide housing for houseless families. POOR Magazine is also preparing to launch Homefulness 2 in Chico/Butte County, the site of recent serious fires.

Radical Redistribution
Dedicated to emergency needs of Po' folks - not related to a specific fund but rather the need of traditionally silenced, criminalized communities in struggle.

What are Community Reparations?

Community Reparations, a concept launched by Lisa "tiny" Gray-Garcia, is rooted in the notion of Interdependence. It's meant to be a healing medicine of resistance to the lie of independence and the separation nation, which encourages the violent act of looking away from people who are poor or unhoused.

Community Reparations instructs us all to resist capitalism's normalizing of separateness and "success" through land-stealing and wealth-hoarding. Instead, Community Reparations recognizes our shared humanity and invites those of us who benefit from stolen or hoarded resources to engage in loving, radical redistribution of these resources.

The Bank of Community Reparations is a national fund of redistributed and stolen wealth that is distributed equally among poor and indigenous people-led land use projects. Resources redistributed to the Bank of Community Reparations may be designated to funds listed -->

To be a part of this crucial act of humanity visit: poormagazine.org/rev.donor.

For more information on Revolutionary Giving to the Bank of Reparations, call (510) 435-7500 or email poormag@gmail.com. To register for the next PeopleSkool Seminar (offered twice a year) for folks with Race/Class Privilege, or set up a set up a training, presentation, talk or individual conversation at your workplace, organization, or community email deeandtiny@gmail.com or go online to www.racepovertymediajustice.org or www.poormagazine.org.

What does Reparations mean to you?
Voices from the POOR Magazine Solidarity Family

"Doing the learning/unlearning work to understand how resource and land acquisition has been maintained culturally/ideologically as well as politically... Giving back and building relationships of support... Being a part of community and interdependence building and learning."
—Julian

"Reparations is active and is meant to help mend past/present/future wounds. It's a responsibility to the interdependence of earth and her residents. It's also seeing that my privilege has been precisely in being able to look away/disconnecting, and so reparations looks like having the hard conversations with family members about this stuff, and not avoiding."
—Miyuki

"I've always tried to be generous with sharing my resources. I haven't had a lot of money in the last 4-5 years. I do things like cook for people and drive people places. Reparations looks like mama giving money or other donations to churches and charities. Her way of showing gratitude for the abundance she has."
—Sandra

"Reparations are a way to heal and to repair broken connections and relationships with those who have been harmed by racism, capitalism, violence, and resource extraction. Reparations have deepened my relationships, and also make it clear that not all indigenous people left the area. This process has led to the formation of some of my closest relationships."
—Cynthia

"Naming the harm that I've caused or benefit from, doing what I can to respond to that harm with material resources that mitigate it."
—Jessica

"When we minimize the impact of slavery or of Native genocide or of the Chinese Exclusion Act or any other example of racism and oppression—we are lying. If your reaction to systems of oppression that you materially benefit from is anything other than wanting—truly wanting—to redistribute resources to mitigate that oppression—then you are lying to yourself about reality, and you will never get a chance to admit that you are human, or experience your own humanity. Reparations are the gateway from lies to life."
—Toby

"Reparations is a process of building relationships and connections to redistribute all kinds of access, knowledge, and skills in addition to financial resources. Reparations is what happens when folks with privilege use it to undermine the systems that exclude people in the first place. It comes from a place of compassion and responsibility, not guilt. It is doing what needs to be done because it is the right thing to do."
—A.S.

"Reparations means making up for past wrongs that my family, ancestors, and I have financially benefited from. It means that every dollar that sits in my bank account and every dollar that I spend is a dollar that cannot be accessed by folks of color. It means that I cannot be whole while I have access to wealth and others do not. Reparations are an opportunity for me to get free."
—Paige

POVERTY SCHOLARSHIP

POOR PEOPLE-LED THEORY, ART, WORDS, & TEARS ACROSS MAMA EARTH

LISA "TINY" GRAY-GARCIA, DEE GARCIA, AND THE POOR MAGAZINE FAMILY

Get a copy of **Poverty Scholarship** (2019) at poorpress.net

Bank of CommUnity Reparations Mamafesto

Words from the POOR Magazine Solidarity Family

Releasing is love.
Enables accountable relationship.
I can sleep at night.
I can love myself.
I can live and be as my whole self.
Joy.
Community.
To be free-er, less held captive by this money.
Live into who I want to be, not requiring myself to be what I
*   was born as.*
Exercise self-determination for myself, and want that and
*   work towards that for others.*
Learn new ways of being, and of safety.

The only safety is community safety
The only freedom is collective freedom
The only future is humanity's future
The current system tells us that with money we as individuals
*   can have safety and freedom and look forward to our*
*   future only if we prioritize ourselves over everyone else*
Meanwhile the world burns
Do I want to be Jeff Bezos on a dick rocket?
Or do I want to be part of our collective future?

I believe my ancestors want me to remember where I come
*   from*
Return to land-based ways of being—which require
*   interdependence and redistribution of resources.*
I believe that in an ableist world I must be deepy intentional
*   about giving where I have capacity and building family to*
*   support me*

We all need support but we have to build support systems that center those most impacted.

Listen, trust, and follow the leadership of poor people and others most impacted by these systems that need to change.
Feel into the abundance in my community, my family, and myself.
Lean into risk—take on more and more risk.
No being perfect.
Move towards family.
Reparations for harms by my people = healing for my people and my ancestors. Return the stolen money to Black, Indigenous, and poor people.

Honesty. Truth.
Capitalism and white supremacy told me a lot of lies.
They told me I was the best, worth more, but not worth anything unless I excelled, played my role, achieved perfection, get it right all the time.
They created a shell of a self and left some hollow parts inside.
I'm claiming my humanity and confronting the parts that want to hide, shy away.
I'm learning how to move in a way that's connected and real.
Real about who I am and where I come from and how I got here and whose backs my ancestors and I stepped on along the way.
Real about my humanity and my interconnectedness with all humans and what that means for my soul and for the dollars in my bank account.

Radical redistribution and distribution
everybody should be involved, connected.
I think that's how it should be framed
Through that connectedness there isn't a me to you
you to me
better/worse

anything at all.
It's about working together in the ways that we are connected
    to each other.
Not anyone feeling guilty, donating money, and then being on
    their way.
It is an ongoing thing that will look different at different stages
a continuing journey.

My mom always said if something is overwhelming break it
    down into steps and do one at a time
Tiny says don't cogitate forever- you have to act on it
We will keep doing steps one by one
We will keep going

Co-written by Solidarity Family members

Community Reparations

CommUnity Reparations is a concept launched by Lisa Tiny Gray-Garcia rooted in the notion of interdependence. It is a healing medicine of resistance to the lies of independence and the separation nation, which frame success as land stealing, wealth hoarding, building lives separated from family and community and, in the process, engaging in the violent act of looking away from people who are poor or unhoused. These lies harm all of us. CommUnity Reparations recognizes our shared humanity and offers a path forward by instructing those of us who benefit from stolen or hoarded resources to engage in loving, radical redistribution of these resources.

The POOR Magazine Community Reparations model is taught to and shared with other poor and Indigenous peoples movements who would like to start their own version of homefulness. Folks with race, class, and/or formal education privilege who are interested in redistributing or reparating are invited to redistribute their resources to the Bank of Community Reparations and/or attend PeopleSkool's Decolonization/DegentriFUKation Seminar to learn more and connect their reparations journey with community.

The following is an overview of what POOR Magazine's CommUnity Reparations model looks like for people with race, class, and/or formal education privilege. CommUnity Reparations is rooted in collective liberation and community, and it looks different in practice for each person. Each of us holds complex identities, lived experiences, and constellations of privilege that influence how we engage in reparations. The stories of community reparators at the end of this section speak to some of the different ways it can look to live CommUnity Reparations and the questions that can come up along the way.

Bank of Community Reparations

Radical redistribution is the foundation of CommUnity Reparations. Radical redistribution asks those of us with access to resources to examine how we came to have access to these resources in the first place. Were these resources accumulated personally or generationally through the theft of land or through labor from Indigenous people, Black people, people of color, and/or poor people? Were these resources accumulated through skills or social connections that were accessed through white supremacy or formal education—institutions that have excluded poor people and people of color from accessing these same resources? Community Reparations names these resources "blood-stained dollars" in recognition of the fact that they were accumulated, whether directly or indirectly, by constraining, harming, and taking the lives of Indigenous people, Black people, poor people, and people of color.

Radical redistribution is grounded in the reality that, for those of us with access, these blood-stained dollars were never ours to begin with. Redistribution, then, is not an act of philanthropy, charity, or gift-giving. Rather, it is an act of returning what has been stolen. It is not about generosity or being a good person. It is also not about guilt or shame. Radical redistribution is rooted in our shared humanity. Radical redistribution recognizes that the accumulation of blood-stained dollars does spiritual harm to the humanity of those who accumulate them and benefit from them, in addition to the multiplicity of harms done to those on whose backs they are accumulated. Further, radical redistribution is a path toward reconnecting with our shared humanity. CommUnity Reparations teaches that radical redistribution, as an act of love, turns blood-stained dollars into love-stained dollars.

The Bank of Community Reparations is a national fund, run by POOR Magazine, into which stolen resources are returned and redistributed equally among poor and Indigenous people-led land use projects. Resources redistributed to the Bank of Community Reparations may be designated to these specific funds:

Po' Mamaz Reparations Fund

Dedicated to redistributing resources directly to poor, unhoused, and formerly unhoused single mamaz (fathers) and children who are unable to afford rent, a drivable vehicle, diapers, food, and other emergency needs related to their survival and thrival.

Tech Reparations Fund

Dedicated to building/preserving the equity of poor and working class communities who have been displaced or are at risk of displacement due to the presence of tech industries and their employees.

Homefulness Community Reparations Fund

Dedicated to building, launching, and growing homefulness comm-UNITIES across Mama Earth. Homefulness is a self-determined landless people's solution to the housing crisis. POOR Magazine is currently in the process of constructing a multi-unit housing complex in East Oakland to provide housing for houseless families. POOR Magazine is also preparing to launch Homefulness 2 in Chico/Butte County, the site of recent, serious fires.

Radical Redistribution

Dedicated to emergency needs of Po folks. It is not related to a specific fund but rather the need of traditionally silenced, criminalized communities in struggle.

Resources can be redistributed to the Bank of CommUnity Reparations through Venmo: @POOR-Magazine

CommUnity Reparations in Action

CommUnity Reparations challenges those of us with race, class, and/ or formal education privilege to liberate not just stolen wealth and blood-stained dollars but also (a) the skills and connections we have accumulated through access to formal education and social networks and (b) the free time that these privileges afford. Doing so also provides an opportunity to un-learn a lot of the colonized ideas about work that some of us have learned in the halls of akkkademia. For example, un-learning the need to get things right or perfect and instead learning how to show up with whatever we've got. Un-learning ideas that we should be "volunteering" to do things that are sexy, stimulating, and ego-boosting, and instead, learning how to roll up our sleeves and do the monotonous, time-consuming stuff that is actually needed but that Poverty Skolaz don't have time for. Un-learning the expectation that tasks will be organized, clear, and linear, and instead, learning how to jump into whatever's needed and figure it out together.

Liberating skills, connections, and labor at POOR can take a lot of shapes and at this time looks like:

Solidarity Family

The Solidarity Family is a community of people with race, class, and/or formal education privilege who have attended POOR Magazine's People Skool seminar over the years and maintain an ongoing relationship as mentees of POOR. With Tiny's mentorship, we meet for regular phone calls on zoom to check in and build community, continue our learning, reflect through writing and discussion, and discuss updates and needs at POOR. This can often be a way to figure out where to plug in and take on tasks that need to be done. There are over 100 people on the Solidarity Family list and we drop in at regular calls when we can.

Admin Team

The Admin Team is a small group of Solidarity Family mentees who are holding down many of the central admin tasks listed below. The admin team meets weekly via phone/Zoom to coordinate. At times many of the admin team's tasks have been held down by one person.

However, when more people have the capacity to collectively hold the admin work it makes for a much smoother and more sustainable process.

Writer Facilitation

Writer Facilitators are paired with Poverty Skola authors who are writing books for POOR Press. Their role is to help bring the book to fruition in the author's vision. This may look like supporting the writing process, copy editing, navigating tech issues, formatting images, and creating a timeline for the book. Writer facilitators attend POOR Press class and meet with the authors outside of class.

Legal Team

The legal team meets to track, strategize, and advocate for legislation as well as deal with and advocate around taxes, permits, and property tax exemptions. The legal team works in partnership with lawyers from The Sustainable Economies Law Center and meets every other week to coordinate.

Tour Support

A small group of Solidarity Family mentees support POOR with logistical support for Stolen Land/Hoarded Resources Un-tours, which share the work of POOR outside of Huichin/the so-called Bay Area. Tasks for tour support include booking rooms and rental cars, coordinating meetings and taking notes, reaching out to organizations, doing WeSearches, making flyers, and helping with social media. These meetings typically happen on a weekly basis leading up to the tour for about 1-2 months.

Work on the Ground

Below is an overview of tasks that are held and taken up by the admin team, solidarity family members, and other mentees:

Communications: Sending out a weekly newsletter, entering new subscribers from events, end of year mailing, and donor communication and organization (google drive database, donor packets, IRS letters and thank you's to donors, cancelling donors).

Events and Gigs: Coordinating and offering rides, updating calendars, outreach for events, updating databases after events, and Zoom support during events.

Finances: Paying bills as they come in, supporting with record keeping for bills, and transferring POOR's Paypal account income to POOR's bank account.

Homefulness: Purchasing appliances and building permits for Homefulness Building Project, tracking relevant legislation, and filing for Alameda County tax exemption each year.

Media: Writing press releases and getting media coverage for advocacy issues.

Office Supplies/Maintenance: Buying office supplies and yearly cleaning of filing cabinets and offices.

PeopleSkool: Compiling and publishing curriculum online, sending out PeopleSkool informational emails and fielding questions from attendees, adding participants to database, and providing Zoom support during PeopleSkool.

POOR Press Store: Working with Poverty Skolaz and their writing, writer facilitation, copy editing, supporting with technical skills like Photoshop for book creation, tracking orders from website, packaging and shipping books to fulfill orders, managing customer relations/payment issues/refunds, and tracking sales to pay out Poverty Skolaz authors.

Publications: Publishing Stories on POOR website and translating publications.

Radical Redistribution: Sending money from Bank of CommUnity Reparations to Poverty Skolaz and gathering or shopping for physical resources (PPE, food, etc.) to be redistributed at POOR Magazine's Thursday market.

Radio: Posting episodes to Soundcloud and supporting with radio maintenance.

Taxes: Preparing and gathering tax documents and entering financial information into QuickBooks.

Tech and Website Maintenance: Checking the website to make sure URLs stay current.

Publications/Notes from the Inside: Picking up letters that come in from plantation prisons, sending back responses from templates, typing up work, editing, and publishing on POOR for Notes from the Inside.

Impromptu Support: Being available for last-minute/impromptu needs.

A Note about Accountability

Many of us with race, class and/or formal education privilege are often accustomed to working within clear structures of accountability that we can plug into and out of as we desire. For example, taking or leaving a volunteer or paid job with clearly defined roles to move into organizational structures that hold the work when we decide to move on. In doing reparations work with POOR, these accountability structures come not from a job description, a paycheck, or a resume builder but from our internal commitment to CommUnity Reparations. It's important to be mindful of our own patterns around accountability, and to take on only what we know we can commit to. Because when we drop the ball, it lands on the backs of Poverty Skolaz and can leave POOR in a crisis. This is why taking on this work also involves a commitment to support with transitions and train new mentees to pick up where we leave off.

Living CommUnity Reparations

CommUnity Reparations instructs those of us with race, class, and/ or formal education privilege to liberate blood-stained dollars, time, labor, skills, and ourselves. This starts with asking hard questions and these questions will look different for each person depending on our identities and the privileges we hold. If my family has hoarded wealth, how did they accumulate it? What extractive industries and/or racist policies made this possible, and how have those same industries and policies harmed Black, Indigenous, and poor people and communities? What have I had access to in my life because of extractive industries and oppressive systems, such as akkkademia or white supremacy, and how have these same systems harmed Black, Indigenous, and poor people? Who are my ancestors, and what is my relationship to them? How have the lies of capitalism and the separation nation come between me and my family, culture, community, and what have I/we lost as a result? How have the lies of capitalism and the lie of independence dictated my ideas of success, and how have they dictated how I move in the world and in relationship with the people in my life?

Living community reparations begins with these inquiries into the real impacts of capitalism and our personal and ancestral actions on Black, Indigenous, and poor communities, and also on our families, communities, and ourselves. We have to be grounded in that truth in order to find new ways. Living Community Reparations is an ongoing process of exploring new ways of being and new questions. How can I connect to the people I come from—my ancestors and my family—with deep love, while naming and accounting for the harms we have participated in and benefitted from? What does that look like for me in my life circumstances? How many of the blood stained dollars I have access to can I turn into love-stained dollars through radical redistribution? What does that stir up in me and what does that liberate in me? How can I redistribute my time and energy to poor people-led work? What do I need to let go of—perfectionism, saviorism, other colonized ways of working—in order to move humbly with accountability in this work? What does that stir up in me, and what does that liberate in me? How can I be more connected with

my ancestors, family, and community? What does that look like for me in my life circumstances? What do I need to make peace with or understand in myself, and in what ways can I engage with my people to be in stronger connection with who I come from? What parts of myself—my self worth and humanity—do I need to honor and claim in order to live community reparations?

Asking and living into these questions can be hard, uncomfortable, beautiful, and liberatory. It is central to making Community Reparations more than a one-time donation or a volunteer stint, but a way of life and a path toward collective liberation and healing.

Stories from CommUnity Reparators

We need community. We need interdependence. We need abundance. We need to grow together. We do not need isolation, fear, or scarcity. We do not need wealth-hoarding.

My family hoards wealth. Most people hoard wealth because of what-ifs. What if we need something? What if there's an emergency? What if we get sick? But as a community, those aren't what-ifs, they're alarm bells. We are sick. We are in an emergency. We all need something. We need homes and food and medicine, all of us. We need education and self-determination, all of us. We need healing, all of us.

Those what-ifs whisper to me too, and I have listened to them, choosing to keep hoarded wealth "just in case." I've let myself be led by the capitalist messages of you-need-this-for-yourself. I'm still learning to walk side-by-side. We will always still be learning. This is a lifelong journey. We will learn to grow together. We will learn to be in solidarity.

POOR Magazine has encouraged me to reconnect with my roots for which I am so grateful. Some Jewish learning—"The assumption underlying all of the gifts to the poor is that these are God's gifts to the poor and not the gifts of the owner of the field… The poor are entitled to be fed because God has given them this food, and the owner of the field is God's steward in this transaction. The owner of the field must transform this duty in as transparent and easy a fashion as possible, free from deception or intimidation, no matter how tempting the produce or its profits may be. If the owner of the field fails in this duty of giving the poor their due, he has essentially stolen another's property."—*Gifts for the Poor, Moses Maimonides' Treatise on Tzedakah,* Rabbi Joseph B. Meszler

Yael Chanoff

As a person with wealth and access to land, it is a necessary step towards healing and solidarity with poor people led movements to move wealth where I can. Capitalism and white supremacy seek to divide us. We must recognize that reparations are one of the radical ways we can act in interdependence and vulnerability with one another. Rather than operating from scarcity, starting with abundance allows us to imagine so many more possibilities. It can be difficult navigating family relationships, especially when they are connected with access to wealth and land, but they can also be points of transformation.

Fei Mok

I'm still learning a lot about being in right relationship as a white person that experiences many privileges. I remember reading in a zine 7 years ago how white folx really need to be taking **at least** 8% of any income and redistributing it to BIPOC communities. At the time I read that I didn't have a job. I was "traveling" and living with family/friends with maybe $100 and an ebt card. This was a relatively short period of my life and for the past 5 years with a stable job, it was something I'd "budgeted" for. Not until recently have I taken steps to move beyond my own personal efforts. I have been helping to mobilize others (mostly white folks) to also redistribute income/wealth and finding ways to grow that 8%. I've focused more on how I am "walking the walk" before I ask family members and friends to do so. I'm grateful to be in community with others where I get to learn more about redistribution, especially to poor-led movements and how to be in solidarity in as many ways as possible. I really appreciate these quotes below. I feel they swiftly describe a sentiment of why reparations and redistribution of wealth are so important.

"Reparations is not aid; it is not a gift; it is compensation to correct the injustices of the past and restore equity."
—Gaston Browne

"Train yourself toward solidarity and not charity. You are no one's savior. You are a mutual partner in the pursuit of freedom."
—Brittany Packnett Cunningham

Lately, I've been thinking about how this happens within capitalism. Like, oh if I work more hours or take this extra job, then I can give more money away. I don't want to perpetuate what can feel like overwork/productivity culture. And also, if I do take this extra job, who am I preventing from taking that opportunity? These are my thoughts in progress, more to come. Thank you.

Kendra Cooley

Sometimes I walk, and sometimes I stumble. Then there are times when I crawl, and times when I roll. When my mother could no longer walk, she realized that she could get further with a wheelchair. I think

of my mother often when I feel the hyper-individualistic desire to try to do everything on my own. Her wheelchair gave her the freedom to move when her legs could no longer support her.

It seems that this can apply to reparations as well. When I cannot walk, I might need assistance to transport me to where I am going. Rather than trying to do everything on my own, I think of the role of community (although not the lie of community that is so often espoused in pseudo-progressive white-dominated spaces by people who never seem to show up when it counts). We do this work of reparations together, and we sometimes carry (or at least support) each other along the way. That is the beauty of what POOR is creating, and I am grateful to be part of this powerful work.

Cynthia Beard

To me, reparations is about doing something with the unearned access I have to resources. As someone who comes from multiple generations of stolen/hoarded wealth on my dad's side, I have a responsibility to make sure the resources my family has used to pay into the American dream get redistributed. Where I am in my life is a product of my privilege. Being able to leave my unsafe home environment and still be housed is directly related to my relationships to people with privilege that I built in college. Going to college on the other side of the country from my family was a result of hoarded wealth. Reparations is about acknowledging that I have a responsibility to shift my ways of being away from myself and everything that colonial values have taught me and towards my people in the struggle. I need to listen to and honor my ancestors who were poor. What right do I have to perpetuate violence against poor people when everything I have is a result of violence against poor people? Connecting to my ancestors and culture means learning about my role in upholding violent systems and centering the people who are impacted by those systems. By redistributing wealth, I can acknowledge my role and do something with my privilege.

Akkkademic Reparations: What does academic reparations look like to you personally in terms of personal access and privilege?

- Supporting others with the skills I have learned, especially organizational privilege and linguistic domination skills.
    - So far this has looked like supporting others in accessing/navigating these institutions and doing admin support.
    - I also need to actively invest in learning the languages of my ancestors. Ideas around "success" and akkkademia are what prevented me from learning in the first place.
- Actively unlearning things I was taught in college, specifically being intentional about how I learn from poor folks and pay for that learning and sharing what I learn with people in my life who also went thru akkkademia.
- Sharing connections I made at school with others.
- Talking to my mama/people in my life about the ways akkkademia is fucked up and oppressive.
- Looking more into the institutions I have benefitted from and the fucked up things they are doing. The stolen land/ hoarded resources tour at UC Berkeley gave some idea of what that could look like.

Maya Ram

Even white, Disabled, Poverty Scholars can live a life of reparations. In fact, we MUST. It is how we can reclaim our humanity. Reparations heal traumas, current and historical, and heal Momma Earth. I've been hustling to get my family and my immediate needs met since I was a small child. I know now that every skill I acquired by standing in social security lines and food bank lines, liberating food from dumpsters or loading docks, and being formerly unhoused are skills that can be put to use and shared to get, not just my needs but, other folks' needs met.

I have heard many women who are Black Power Movement builders and Black, Brown, and Indigenous people who lost their loved ones to poLice violence say—white people need to weaponize every privilege they have for our collective liberation. That really resonates with me. I revisit that often and brainstorm more ways I can be active in reparations work. Sometimes the most important life work I do is connecting two people and getting out of the way. I am often like a stream between two bodies of water, opening up a flow so people can get needs met. Weaponizing privilege means every time I travel somewhere, I make sure another Black, Indigenous, Poverty Scholar also gets to travel. I might have to fundraise for my own travel or ask my community for support. Now, I ask at least double. I'm leveraging my social capital, my partner privilege in that work.

I am an artist. I make short movies. I write. I chalk sidewalks. I can do all those things FOR COLLECTIVE LIBERATION.

I don't love fundraising, but I'm good at it. I am literally almost always holding down or lifting up at least one online fundraiser. Online fundraisers are the mainstream language and I see these "fundraisers" as opportunities for radical redistribution. Holding down online "fundraisers" all the time is not sustainable, and it's what I have access to. They are a way to get folks' immediate needs met. It's a gift that folks trust me to hold down an online fundraiser when they are in need. It's a responsibility that I have, that people who are resourced look to me for places to redistribute money. I can't hand someone $2500 for first months rent and deposit, but I can make sure it gets raised.

Reparations is not "I gave at the office." It's forever work. It means having cash on me so if I see an unhoused neighbor and they ask me for cash I can give it to them.

Much of my Life's Work has become tending land, even the small square of "rented" land I live on. I am in reparations relationship with Ancestors and Momma Earth.

Lisa Ganser

For me, practicing reparations is a commitment to my own healing and the healing of my ancestors. I am with Aime Cesaire who said that anyone who participates in the brutalization of anyone else becomes themselves a brute. I believe that my family's participation in land and labor theft and the ongoing oppression of Black and indigenous people has made us spiritually sick and in need of healing. I work toward that healing by contributing money, time, and energy toward liberation movements led by BIPOC people. It gives back far more than I give.

Nichola Torbett

To me, reparations means:

- Rejecting the cult of individuality and embracing our shared humanity and interdependence; fighting the narratives of independence and self-sufficiency that I have been conditioned to hold
- Learning the true history and nature of this land and this country, recognizing the genocide and exploitation that it was founded on and the exploitative system of racial capitalism that it runs on to this day
- Leveraging my privilege, resources, and access to work towards "repair" of historical injustice, inequity, poverty, extraction => for me this means my skills/network/privilege/access as a tech worker and as a college-educated wealthy white woman.
- I have a technical degree from an "elite" institution, which I was able to obtain debt-free because of my family's wealth, and which has in turn given me access to job security and

high-paying work. Academic reparations isn't a phrase I've heard before, but I think to me it looks like:

- Contributing and sharing my specialized technical skills (and wealth accumulated based on these skills) to support organizations that are focused on fighting oppression and/or serving their communities
- Advocating for equitable/universal access to higher education and/or specialized technical training
- Challenging the idea that professionalism & "business English" are prerequisites for legitimacy
- Respecting all people as experts on their own lived experience
- Deferring to oppressed peoples as experts on the systems that oppress them

Emily Bram

My work with POOR has looked different over the years. I started by going to People Skool, which at that time was a multi-week program with an internship. At that time, it was an 8-week program but graduation kept getting pushed back and our internship kept going, which was one of the first lessons. I remember that when I first started People Skool, I was determined to set myself apart from other rich kids. I was gonna be different, I was gonna be a cool rich kid not a regular rich kid. I was gonna get it right and impress all the Poverty Scholars. Turns out, that is like one of the most typical (and arrogant) rich kid attitudes out there. And learning humility and vulnerability has been the greatest gift I've received from POOR. Poverty Scholars aren't surprised when even the coolest rich kids slip up into habits of entitlement, perfectionism, flakiness, etc. And they still invite us to participate. Once I realized that I was amazed. Wow, POOR really is here for the healing, there is not an extractive orientation to class privileged people. It's not give us your money and time and see you later. Often, it actually slows Poverty Scholars down to include us in the work, but it's a conscious, political choice about healing and transformation.

In terms of roles, I did one-off admin tasks that have sometimes been site-based. This included things like mailings, data entry, cleaning up lists, phone banking, miscellaneous admin duties, errands, etc. Also, I gave rides to deecolonize academy scholars. That was my favorite part, listening to the kids in the van. I've done some writer facilitation on articles with Poverty Scholars, and that's also been one of my favorite memories of doing work with POOR. Since leaving the Bay Area, I worked with the local community in Tennessee where I was living at the time to bring POOR to our community. With a team of local folks and working closely with POOR and Bay Area Solidarity Family members in the Bay, I did logistical support, holding relationships, getting people paid, and general fundraising.

That makes it seem like I did a lot but it was spread over 10 years and there were years I did very little. One thing I see people minimizing and overlooking as a contribution is showing up at events—being a body in the room, ears for listening—like showing up at community news room even if you don't take on a task.

One thing I struggled with was over-promising and under-delivering, and that's one of the big cross-class pitfalls I see in reparators. People over-promise and under-deliver which is then followed by shame. This leads to avoiding POOR and eventually dropping out. But avoidance doesn't make shame go away. I've certainly done things over the years with POOR that I felt ashamed of.

At one point I was giving $500 a month and POOR was using that money to feed maybe 100 people a week. In the meantime I was having bad boundaries with money with friends who were struggling with housing, and I had the idea that it's better for me to give money to working class people I know directly rather than a non-profit organization that could get grants somewhere else. I stopped giving that money to POOR and gave it to my friend who was in crisis without communicating about it with POOR. Tiny called me and we had what was for me a really hard conversation where she really spelled out how that had impacted the organization and the people in it, including herself. I'm used to money coming with anonymity and privacy, or general sketchiness around money. I was being sketchy but I wasn't able to hide in my sketchiness. It felt like the biggest gift was for Tiny to not just write me off as another asshole who didn't get it, but as a family member who had caused harm and could learn and change. It really changed my relationship with POOR, to realize I was still wanted as part of the family even if I did something pretty seriously wrong. That honesty is what heals shame. From there, I decided to give in ways I can sustain, not give as a monthly contribution if it's really a one-time contribution, etc.

I started to under-promise and over-deliver with my time too, trying to honor my own needs more. I expected a lot of pushback about having boundaries and I realized that that was mostly projection. A lot is asked from us, but Poverty Scholars tend to not have the sense of entitlement that is ubiquitous in the communities I'm from. So, even if a lot is asked, no one is expected to say yes to anything that's too much for them. For those of you who are like me with the tendency to want to fix, save, solve, and stand apart as a super achiever or what have you, we have to challenge ourselves to say I'm not gonna be able to do that or I need help. Three very powerful words, "I need help." At POOR, the message is you're not here to perform. We're here to help you as much as you're here to help us. When you're being a perfectionist we're here to remind you, just show up with what you've got, even if what you've got are needs. This is where the healing begins.

Toby Kramer

Hoarded wealth tries to make itself invisible. *Look away*, it says, *there's nothing to see here.* It accumulates in the shadows of other people's exploitation and pretends it's innocent and normal and natural and good. It was always there, hiding in plain sight—in my grandparents' garage with three Porsches (and the joke-lie that we're not rich, that all the money in this family just gets turned into cars), in the $2,000 checks every birthday and Christmas, in the investments and education savings accounts in my name since my birth, my complete lack of student or other loans—thinly camouflaged behind my mom's tight budgeting and frugality and worrying about our collective financial futures. I grew up internalizing its lies: "We're middle class—comfortable, but not wealthy."

Middle-class mythology requires a kind of self-deception that can only remain intact as long as you refuse to look the reality of wealth in the face. I've only learned how to see my family's hoarded wealth for what it is through relationships with poor people-led movements. My parents are solidly managerial class. Several years ago, my mom "confided" in me that their net worth is much more than she thought it was and told me explicitly not to tell anyone the exact amount—to keep the hoarded wealth invisible. My grandparents on both sides are undoubtedly upper class. Their wealth is no longer invisible to me, but it's still undefined. They guard its secrets closely, teasing at it with jokes about inheritances and vague offers of infinite support.

I'm endlessly grateful that my parents are loving, compassionate, principled people, and that my close relationship with them has allowed me to bring them along this unlearning & relearning journey with me. I've learned that their love for me can also translate into support for the people I care about too. I'm still working on passing along the

fundamental concepts of radical redistribution and community reparations as taught by POOR, but I know that even getting this far is the
beginning of healing our generational patterns of wealth-hoarding.
In the meantime, I've been able to leverage my relatives' willingness
to give me money so that I can get it to where it needs to go. When I
temporarily lost my job due to COVID and was unable to get unemployment benefits for months, my grandmother dropped $5000 into
my account with no questions asked. I did need some of it to cover
my portion of rent for those months, but the rest I funneled directly to
Black trans folks in my mutual networks, with some of it set aside for
ongoing support so that I can be a consistent and sustainable source
of reparatory giving.

My biggest source of struggle in reparations work right now is
the uncertainty of "the future." The scripts I learned about saving for
retirement, not dipping into my savings, etc. are so deeply embedded
in me. I work a low-paying job because I can afford to, but I still don't
know how to reconcile being low-income for the entirety of my fore-
seeable career with having access to significant generational wealth.
All I have are questions.

How do I weigh the potential for future personal need against the reality of ongoing, constant, critical need of others around me? What does it mean to have "enough" in a world hell-bent on endless accumulation? What's the point of saving for "retirement" in a world that seems like it's sprinting toward its own destruction? Am I just expecting being a class traitor to be a comfortable process?

I get lost in these questions often, and I'm still fumbling for clarity. The specificity and transparency of other folks with hoarded wealth privilege feels like it gives me footholds in the midst of something made so intentionally murky for centuries ("It's not polite to talk about money"). I appreciate the openness of everyone who has moved toward reparations for themselves, and the guidance of the poor folks who have given so much guidance and grace and honesty to all of us.

In the meantime, I practice reparations in other ways too. Hoarded wealth privilege has given me so much more than literal money—skills, connections, academic language, etc. My time and labor have been shaped by my class status, and I can and do use them as reparatory offerings as well.

A.S. Ikeda

Chapter 5
Tools for Mama Earth Liberation

Checklist for Poverty Skolaz MamaFesting Homefulness

1 Writing Theatre/ Visioning Workshops with houseless/poor/ indigenous poverty skolaz (help provided by POOR Magazine)

2 Poverty Skola Meeting with Tiny over phone/zoom email

3 Collection/Organizing of People with race, class, formal education

4 Attendance by poverty skolaz and peoples with privilege in PeopleSkool

5 Creation of Rules of Respect and MamaFesto for Change decided among your poverty skola members

6 Commitment session from Bank of ComeUnity Reparations and conscious wealth-hoarders from your territory to form a "branch" of the Bank of Comeunity Reparations in your area

7 Prayer and protocol meetings with 1st Nations/aboriginal/indigenous land stewards of your stolen/colonized Mama Earth

8 How To Not Call PoLice workshop with POOR Magazine and all of your members

9 Establishment of "Branch" in your city or town of Bank of ComeUnity Reparations with help from POOR Magazine Solidarity family

10 Secure Commitment of Resources for "Purchase" of Mama Earth in your area from the newly formed Branch of the Bank of ComeUnity Reparations in your area or Donation of Land already "owned"

11 Revolutionary Real Estate Broker/Agent acquired in your area

12 Love/Liberation Land Team decided on

13 Search for Mama Earth—Zoning, Research on poisoning of Mama Earth and history/Herstory of MamaEarth

14 "Buying" of Land or Legal Memorandum Of Understanding (MOU) with existent "Land-Stealers/Owners" including a

pro-bono or donated services or paid for by privileged people lawyer that includes deed restriction and agreement for Indefinte use agreement or Land Liberation agreement

15 Prayer, Permission and Protocol with 1st Nations communities and request for prayer of the Mama Earth you aquire

16 Permit gangster/Zoning research- what in your Settler colonized town or city is required to "build" (they are always different)

17 Acquisition of Architect/Engineer/Designer pro-bono

18 Removal of Asphalt, Concrete,or other forms of cleaning, loving preparing

19 Community Visioning sessions on the land and Love offerings in that area for the existent communities- food, prayer, healing- speaking out—outreach- (fo rus this mean the establishment of a Sliding Scale Cafe but can also be just a visioning session— ComeUnity Gardens for EVERYONE in the ComeUnity who wants food

20 Revolutionary Building Circles and design sessions and final design agreed on

21 Building /MamaFesting Resources to begin the plan

22 Plans submitted to Zoning

23 Community Organizing of the community to support you

24 Reaching out to Poltricksters in your district- They dont have to like you- but you are letting them know

25 Outreach to Churches and neighborhood members and more Community Meetings and Garden boxes planted, Murals painted, prayer sessions,—and/or other community activities

26 Possible Crowd Sourcing for Building Budget in addition to whatever Bank of ComeUnity Reparations Branch can raise

27 Peoples Agreement Process Launched with poverty skolaz/future residents.

MamaFesto of Poverty Skolaz to Mama Earth (& Peoples Agreement for Homefulness Residents)

1. I, _____ understand that this herstoric MamaFesto document heretofore known as The Peoples Agreement is rooted in the 525 year struggle of all of the co-founders, residents and future residents who are landless, indigenous, houseless, poor and criminalized peoples who have suffered wite-supremacy, forced diaspora, chattel slavery, border hate,different forms of abuse,violence, removal, gentrification, racism, hatred, incarceration, profiling and/or multiple forms of systems/institutional abuse in this stolen indigenous land the colonizers call the US.

2. I understand that this, The Peoples Agreement, is a sacred document, not held together by armed agents of the state (Po'Lice, Military, etc) but by each other, poor folks, working together, self-determined, with humility, and love.

3. I understand that by signing it, by agreeing to live here on the sacred land we call Homefulness, you are making a commitment to your fellow human, animal and land, to follow the rules of respect stated here, as well as the agreements listed below.

4. I understand that this document is grounded in the Declaration of Inter-dependence created in 2009 at the Revolutionary Change Session and the Manifesto for Change created by Mama Dee & Tiny in 1996 along with Volume 1 of POOR Magazine entitled Homefulness—a poor people-led solution to Houselessness

5. I understand that I/we are stewards of the land—we, the landless, indigenous, poor peoples who live/work/ learn on the land at Homefulness & our children & our children's children and generations beyond—DO NOT OWN MAMA EARTH. None

of us who live here/work here/learn here/heal here "own" the land, but because this land and all of us exist within a capitalist system who will easily take a certain amount of blood-stained dollars to evict us, displace us or remove us—we understand that their needs to be some entity on paper that "owns" the land or it will get stolen by more government gangsters or devil-opers.

    a. Above All, I _____ Understand and am agreeing completely and fully that myself or my family or my descendants have no right to sell any portion of this land or project located on the colonizer map as 8032 Macarthur Blvd, East Oakland, CA 94605

6. As resident you are agreeing to steward/support/love, respect and contribute through blood-stained dollaz and/or poor people sweat-equity or a combination of both equaling a certain amount per month, which is a fluctuating portion of the amount of blood-stained dollars needed for taxes, water, gas, sewer, cable, wi-fi, & other maintenance peoples like plumbers, electricians, etc until we remove ourselves completely from the Blood-stained dollar economy into a purely barter based sharing comeUnity.

    a. *Poor People sweat includes hours per week and month but is not exclusive too: running street news-room, taking care of goats, chickens, cleaning the land, gardening duties, School work, maintenance work on the land to be determined by The Work Collective entity managed by POOR Magazine. Profit/fees taken in by the POOR Magazine Work collective will support POOR Magazine's budget as we have no other funding. Work/maintenance does not include basic stuff like trash being put out in front or basic watering.

    b. Micro-businesses proposals by families who reside here that will take place on the land at Homefulness should be proposed through the Elephant Council and work out some way to off-set/support the Homefulness project. *All families moving in with businesses already in process – please let Homefulness know at the Intergenerational council when you present your family.

7. I understand that I, my family and my families' family are welcome to live here for the rest of their lives, their children's children and their future generations to come. And that every generation who lives here are bound to these same agreements and promises to follow them. And as long as all families' descendents follow the same commitments they will be welcome to be here forever.

8. I understand that if I do not follow one of these agreements, an Intergenerational Council will be called to order where I will be accountable to my fellow residents to explain why and to address what I did, agree to resolutions and figure out solutions.

9. I understand that a maximum of 3 Intergenerational councils will be held per year per person/per family about an issue. The amount of intergenerational councils that will be held will be on a case by case basis based on the issue that comes up. If it is abuse of a child, physical or weapon-based violence to others, sexual violence against anyone, there will only be one intergenerational meeting called. In the case of these aforementioned acts or others being perpetrated by a family or individual or when a family or person has reached their maximum limit of intergenerational meetings needed to be called, the Intergenerational Council has the right to ask you to leave Homefulness.

10. Each family will be responsible for their own children under 18. After 18 the child will be accountable to the Intergenerational council for their actions.

11. As a resident you are agreeing to attend several meetings per month. THIS IS THE WAY ALL THINGS ARE DONE AT HOMEFULNESS.

    a. The bi-weekly Homefulness Elephant Council and Building Circle meetings, plus a monthly Intergenerational Council, Community Newsroom meetings and eventually Work Collective/Healing from Trauma meetings (for all core problems that come up & basic decisions).

    b. All community members who want to propose projects or events need to come to this as well. **Performance/Art/Teaching/Outreach on the revolutionary work that Homefuness was built by to community

12. For Now, Elephant Council meetings will be held to make ALL decisions on the land at Homefulness. After 2016, there will be a Budget Circle that will convene as an offshoot of the Work Collective to MAKE ALL MONEY decisions.

13. Each resident agrees to attend Hoarder/clutterer/Trauma/Addiction/Survival from Isolation Amerikkka Support groups held weekly at first, bi-weekly and/or monthly with youth & adult support teams providing ongoing support to help each of us keep us grounded in love, support, to hold us in this space of trauma and oppression, to provide help to survive together. All of these meetings will be around a dinner hosted by one of the members. If there is no trauma, it's just a dinner with support, love and inter-dependence.

14. Each member agrees to not put belongings outside of home (i.e, bicycles are kept in home, boxes, belongings, stuff are kept in your own space).

15. Each resident agrees to keep their homes clean and organized and not filled with clutter they don't need—and if they are collecting clutter, they agree to seek help from the support

teams for building shelves, offering clothes to the sewing collective, free store, community closet, before a "hoarder clutterer" situation is caused. Also, we have once-a-month Homefulness trips to the dump. All people can help with this and add stuff to the pile. This expense is one of the small expenses we need to calculate in the costs.

16. Each resident agrees to put trash in the bins & rotate with the community on bringing out trash bins to the front street, as well as a list of collective chores to keep the land clean and take care of the land.

17. All families need to help with monthly clean-up of land and areas, and together we can decolonize our mind from individual, default, I-got-mines behavior to inter-dependence. This is also part of pre-move-in training/healing.

18. Each resident understands that if they invite a partner, boyfriend, girlfriend, mother, father, uncle, auntie, daughter or sun, friend or caregiver to live in their home on Homefulness, they are agreeing to have the guest attend a PeopleSkool session before they can become a member of Homefulness and if they stay for longer than two weeks (14 days) in succession they will be asked to attend a session of PeopleSkool and go through the inter-generational council process, ID and Background Check for child safety (only institutional involvement because of child safety first).

19. Each person who comes to the land beyond agrees to the Rules of Respect for residents (see below).

20. Each resident agrees to not use any substance including alcohol, medical marijuana and cigarettes at any public space on the land at Homefulness (agreed, voted and deeply discussed in Inter-generational Council meetings of 2014).

21. Each resident agrees to use only medical marijuana or alcohol or prescribed pharmaceuticals or cigarettes in their own home

(agreed, voted and discussed in Inter-generational Council meetings).

22. People understand that this is a Po'Lice free zone—issues, problems, behavior and egregious violations are not resolved with wite-supremacist agents of the state. All issues are resolved using our model of self-determined accountability—we are all responsible for each other. It is understood that this value is what we hold as an organization for this land, and as a group we will not be calling a police agency to resolve issues. If a person outside our Homefulness family perpetrates harm, threatens violence against us, our children or this land, we will ask our community comrades such as the Black Riders, community elders or other mediating person or group to assist us in reaching a resolution to the issue. As well, we hold the value as a group to not engage with a Po'Lice agency ever, but we cannot prevent an individual from seeking their forms of redress about acts that put them in danger, whatever they may be.

23. We will have chickens for eggs and goats for milk which POOR Magazine will get donations to purchase. POOR Magazine Work Collective will be distributing them between the Homefulness camp for barter of time to the Work Collective, and also as a part of Deecolonize Academy as a learning tool for the children in science and math.

24. There is a limit of three (3) animals per household and any dangerous (pit bulls, rottweilers, other large dogs) animals must be kept in your own space (This is subject to change based on future Inter-generational Council decisions).

25. All traditions of spirit are equally respected. No disparaging insults are made to other people for their practices, as long as they are practiced in an open and respectful manner. The Elephant Council will decide about use of community space for all events in the same manner as everything else.

26. Noise on the land outside of community events or pre-noticed ceremonies needs to be based on basic Rules of Respect to each other as residents (i.e. no parties or loud music before 9 am on weekdays or 10am on weekends and not after 12 midnight on weekends, if you will be having a party or event please let fellow residents know ahead of time, etc.)

27. If there is an issue that comes up or a conflict between the organization and the resident and or between residents, residents agree to seek a resolution through the Homefulness People's Court (before you go to the Man's kkkourt).

28. If we have a problem with someone from outside of the resident circle, we appoint a duo of "problem-solvers" from the group to be the first go-to person to deal with the problem and/or the person's issue.

29. It is understood that some of us who have survived trauma of different kinds will possess weapons in our private residences, which are carefully kept away from their and other minor children under 18. And it is understood that these are for use in our private homes only and not to be used against other residents.

30. If people do leave Homefulness, they agree to still follow rules of respect (i.e. not harassing members in community spaces, not cyber-bullying any POOR family online, etc.)

31. All families who move to Homefulness agree to move here with a 3 month trial run. If it does not work out, new residents agree to leave amicably.

Rules of Respect

Rules of Respect for all public spaces, events, meetings and the land, which will be posted in all buildings and homes.

The following are the rules of respect on the sacred land we call Homefulness. These are subject to change based on other issues that arise.

1. Please do not use perfumes or scented products in public spaces to respect those with asthma in meetings and public spaces.

2. In meetings, please raise your hand when you have an opinion. There is no microphone, so don't talk over someone else.

3. Please be in all public spaces sober. No use of substances including alcohol, pharmaceuticals, medical marijuana or cigarettes.

4. NO guns, knives, or weapons anywhere. We have children here, and we need to ensure their safety before anything else.

5. NO aggressive or violent behavior with other members of our family in this space. Please move with respect and humility. Please do not act with aggression or violence toward anyone on the land. If you get upset, remember there are other ways to handle/resolve issues.

6. If you have problems with someone, if you get angry, feel betrayed or the urge to become aggressive—walk away, leave the meeting and/or call an Inter-generational Council in order to resolve your issue.

7. This is a Po'Lice Free & Devil-oper Free Zone.

8. Please respect people's physical boundaries. No innapropriate touch or sexual harassment of any child or adult anywhere on the land.

9. Please pick up your own trash after you. We are all stewards of this sacred land. Please respect your Mama Earth like you respect your mama.

Boilerplate Project Plan

HOMEFULNESS—a poor and Indigenous people-led solution to Homelessness

A sweat equity, permanent co-housing, education, arts, micro-business, and social change project for landless/houseless and formerly houseless families and individuals.

I. **4-10 Family Housing Units, Multi-Generational School/ Media Center, Community Garden/Farm, and Sliding Scale Cafe**

    Detailed Description: 4-10 Permanent housing units for houseless and formerly houseless families following an Indigenous model of co-housing which includes the following:

    -   A site for Deecolonize Academy/ F.A.M.I.L.Y.(Family Access to Multicultural Intergenerational Learning with our Youth) which is a revolutionary on-site child care and school for houseless children and families. It incorporates a social justice and arts-based, multicultural and multilingual curriculum for families and children ages 2-102;
    -   A site for POOR Magazine, PeopleSKool, The Race, Poverty, and Media Justice Institute, Community Newsroom, and all of POOR's Indigenous community arts programming; and
    -   A site for Uncle Al & Mama Dee's Sliding Scale Cafe, a multi-generational community arts and social justice eating and performance space.

II. **The Space: 8032-8034 MacArthur (BlackArthur) Blvd, (Huchuin Ohlone Land), East Oakland**

    -   An R4 zoned (mixed use) lot in East Oakland.

III. **Funding**

    -   Equity "Capital" Campaign budget: 2.5 million
        -   $200,000 already raised;
        -   Lot purchased and paid in full;

- Phase 1 completed. Existing building was renovated and now houses 3 unhoused families and elders. Also houses Deecolonize Academy;
- Permits from the CIty of Oakland were acquired; and
- Phase 2 (in progress) was launched July 2016.

All remaining fundraising will occur through an Equity campaign launched by POOR Magazine.

As an act of resistance to the hierarchal and unjust distribution of wealth and resources locally and globally, POOR Magazine is formerly calling the fundraising effort for HOMEFULNESS, an Equity Campaign, instead of a Capital Campaign. Through equity sharing, not tied to financial resources, we will be creating permanent and lasting solutions to houselessness for families in poverty who have been displaced, evicted, gentrified, and destabilized out of their Indigenous lands and communities.

For more information on how to become involved with this project, please email deeandtiny@poormagazine.org.

To donate to the Homefulness Project, send checks to:

POOR Magazine
8032 Macarthur Bl
Oakland, Ca 94605

Photo by Bob Theis, an architect whose radical redistribution of resources made Homefulness possible

A.S. Ikeda is a radical redistributor with POOR Magazine's Solidarity Family. They are an artist, book/graphic designer, and editor. See more of their work at **asikeda.com**

Made in the USA
Columbia, SC
29 October 2021

47932963R00148